TV On/Off

TV ON/OFF

Better Family Use of Television

Ellen B. De Franco

Goodyear Publishing Company, Inc.

Santa Monica, California

Library of Congress Cataloging in Publication Data

De Franco, Ellen B
    TV on/off.

    Bibliography: p. 156
    1. Television and children.   2. Television and
family.   I. Title.
HQ784.T4D43   791.45'01'3   80-20776
ISBN 0-8302-9128-8

Copyright © 1980 by
Goodyear Publishing Company, Inc.
Santa Monica, California 90401

Y-9128-3

ISBN: 0-8302-9128-8

Current printing (last digit):
10 9 8 7 6 5 4 3 2 1

Cover and Interior Design: Kenny Beck

Printed in the United States of America

To my children and grandchildren,
who have kept the imaginative world of childhood
open for me.

Contents

Introduction

The incentive to write this book grew on me gradually over the past several years as I listened to my students in both preschool-curriculum and parent-education classes. It was the teachers who first began to comment about changes in the behavior of the children whom they taught. Term after term I heard the same concerns expressed. Briefly, these concerns center around children's growing aggression, apathy, and television-related play. They have the sad proof that many of even the youngest preschoolers are staying up very late, viewing programs neither meant for nor appropriate for young children, and almost *ad nauseum* discussing and acting out at school what they have seen.

Recently one teacher volunteered that a new rule has been made at her school, where two- to five-year-olds attend: no dramatic play based on TV is allowed. The staff is experimenting to see what results from this policy, and an early report indicates that the children's imaginative play is now more creative and original. This is a beginning phase in a long and difficult reeducation plan for the children and *their parents.*

The parents I meet have children of all ages. Consistently in our discussions they express their anxieties about the hold television seems to exert on their families. Their approach to this emotionally loaded subject is far different from that of the teachers. Parent-group discussions usually include a variety of confessions like "He watches TV all the time, but I don't know how to stop him," or "I guess I watch too much so my kids do, too," or "I like to watch the news, and my six year old insists on watching with me. I don't want her to see some of the bad stuff on the news. What should I do with her?'' Feelings of guilt and inadequacy become intermixed, parents are upset, and the majority of them seem at a loss about how to cope. They make small stabs at trying to urge their children to cut down on the hours spent in front of the set. Usually the ensuing struggle is distasteful enough to force them to back down, angry at themselves for this weakness and resentful of the ubiquitous television set that causes the trouble.

I have discovered that all of the parents I see, including those who are not too disturbed about television's intrusion in their family life, are very interested in hearing about the things they can do to ameliorate television's effects. It has amazed me that so many have responded eagerly to my suggestions. Their eagerness often indicates that they are almost desperate to find something to try. Each parent-education course I teach concerns itself more and more with television-related concerns and problems.

And so the motivation for organizing and putting my ideas into book form came from the messages I heard from my students. In this book, I have worked hard to avoid the downbeat, defeatist attitude that so often accompanies mention of children and television today. My conviction is that television's good aspects far outweigh its bad ones. The responsibility for taking the best possible advantage of available programming rests with television's viewers, and in the case of children this responsibility belongs to the adults who are raising and teaching them. I admit that I am apprehensive about the number of poor and unsavory productions polluting the airwaves, but I contend that we who use the medium *do* have the choice to switch channels or to turn off the set. In any one day's schedule there are always worthwhile programs, varied and numerous enough to meet different interests and age levels.

My own reaction to television is optimistic. I am continually impressed with its teaching potential, not only via educational television per se, a boon to children and teachers alike, but also from regular fare. Incredible production skills package information and entertainmment in ways that facilitate learning, making the process effortless and exciting. Compared to the other electronic wonders of our age, television is, I believe, the most promising of all for family benefit. The problem is that most of us have taken it too casually, and in so doing have allowed it to be more of an abusive than a constructive influence.

My wish for improved general programming and more special shows for children is as fervent as anyone else's, but I am realistic enough to recognize that such changes may be minimal and slow to happen. For this reason I emphasize how necessary it is *now* for parents to become much more involved in their families' television use. I believe it is as foolhardy to abandon children to unguided viewing as it would be to give them complete freedom of choice in other areas of their lives. Television has a significant effect on all of us, our children most particularly. We should take it more seriously.

When I first started discussing television and children with parents, I plunged right into practical ideas, not mentioning the dark side. I soon found that this approach was unsuitable. Parents wanted to use the opportunity to pool their experiences and feelings about TV's role in their family life. They were eager to gauge the extent of its impact on their own children by listening to others' accounts of what was happening to theirs. Although admitting it was uncomfortable, they were willing to face the dilemma posed by TV and to make some resolutions about what to do.

The needs of these people with whom I met set the pattern for this book. Under the assumption that those mothers and fathers are typical of most, I opted to mention the bitter with the sweet. Although I have tried to soften a threatening tone as much as I can, I have been unable to gloss over the fact that indiscriminate use and overuse of television can be damaging. I think most people need to become more aware of how powerful this medium is and how relatively little is known about its long-term effects on viewers. I have therefore stated warnings and pleas to my readers for more careful attention to children's television habits. If I had not done this, I would have been less than honest. Often the decision of whether or not to mention a gloomy prognostication was simplified when I realized that it might serve as a precautionary measure. In my opinion, that reason alone seems valid enough to include a discussion of the potential harm of television.

As an antidote to any discouragement parents might feel, I have taken pains whenever possible to list many reasons why and how the activities I suggest can help children. In some instances I have even hinted that adults too can benefit from the same practices, emphasizing the need for family participation in many of them. Although my main goal is to improve family use of television, my secondary one is to offer ideas for upgrading general harmony between parents and children through the activities they do together.

The chapters that follow, then, describe what I call the *TV On/Off Project* (sometimes referred to as the *Project*) for better family use of television. The activities and methods described are simple and practical, and are adaptable to children of different ages and interests. Directions are given for many specific activities, called Helpful Things to Do. I have also included Awareness Activities that are meant primarily as attitude warm-ups for parents.

The first chapter, "The Family in Our TV Society," focuses attention on the impact of television on family life. As television is now an important and constant component of most homes, its probable influence on everyone's attitudes and behaviors must be considered. Readers are encouraged to compare family life today with their recollections of family life in the past, and suggestions are made for enriching family activities. Chapter 2, "TV—A Personal Habit," provides a questionnaire, charts, and other ways to observe the role of TV in each family member's life; for the most successful attempts to alter habits are those adapted individually. The chapter also includes activities to pave the way for family cooperation as the *Project* gets underway.

Chapters 3 and 4 concern the *TV Off* part of the *Project*. Chapter 3, "Recommendation: Some TV Turn Off," describes how parents can most effectively implement the decision to reduce TV watching. Realizing how difficult, if not abhorrent, the thought of watching less TV is to children (adults too!), I have presented various methods of making this more acceptable. Chapter 4, "Winning the Battle against TeeVeeitis," takes up the problem of more serious TV addiction and offers guidance and support for parents who want to ease the family's withdrawal from TV.

The next four chapters concern the *TV On* part of the *Project:* how parents can help their children benefit from, and not be hurt by, the TV they watch. My suggestions in Chapter 5, "Put Heads Together in Front of the Set," are perhaps the easiest to follow. They are based on a common-sense approach to parent-children parallel viewing. My feeling is that in the long run, this is the method most guaranteed to bring success. In Chapter 6, "TV—Springboard for Family Discussions," I show how to apply the same techniques in family talks and activities related to children's reactions to the television they see. These are planned to air and deal with children's misconceptions, confusions, and attitudes about their TV mentors and heroes.

I am under the impression that all TV viewers, young and old alike, underestimate the medium's insidious effect on emotions. I know people can learn to cope with moods evoked once they are aware of and face them. In Chapter 7, "TV—The Emotional Mix-Master," I include simple safety-valve activities that can lessen or stop any excessive anxieties generated by television.

I felt it necessary to write Chapter 8, "Put TV Under the Microscope," because most children know very little about the ins and outs of production, nor do they understand that TV is business, not just entertainment. An analysis of how programs are conceived and made is fascinating, so I took advantage of that fact to combine information with projects for children. These activities cover just about every kind of program currently aired. The more knowledgeable children are about the television industry, the better protected they are against total acceptance of what they see and hear on their sets.

If properly used, television can stimulate children's creativity, and therefore I followed Chapter 8, which concerns analysis of television, with Chapter 9, "Creative Extensions of TV." Once alerted to some of the fabulous craftsmanship of TV, hopefully children will want to try out some of the ideas and techniques used in television. This chapter begins my emphasis on encouraging children to use their own creativity, a childhood characteristic that seems to have taken second place to television viewing. In Chapters 10 and 11, "Forget TV! Other Interesting Things to Do" and "More Creative Replacements for TV," I have devoted a large amount of space to specific writing, art, and music projects. These projects are meant to lead children back to the recreational outlets that were more commonplace before the advent of television.

In Chapter 12, "Far Away from TV—Accentuating Awareness," I have ventured into a realm that is familiar to everyone, although seldom purposefully entered. Today's frenetic life-styles leave little or no time for appreciating small experiences that actually are very valuable—the kind of moments that give lasting pleasure and are the bulwarks of good emotional health. It is during childhood that receptiveness to the wonders of the world are usually keenest. As a change from television's synthetic bag of awareness tricks, I offer down-to-earth, easily achieved ones that are immediately available to everyone.

In Chapter 13, "A Look Ahead: TV in Your Family's Future," I tie up the loose ends of the *TV Turn On/Off Project* by suggesting a postquestionnaire and some ideas for celebrating improvements in the family's use of television. I have also included general guidelines for finding suitable children's programs, as well as mention of national organizations working on behalf of better television for children.

My last chapter, "TV—The Powerful Demon-Angel," briefly summarizes research findings and current opinions about television's impact on children and families. I feel that this kind of information cannot be omitted from my book, but I realize that it is difficult to read with equanimity. I hope this chapter will convince my readers that intervention in children's television viewing is an essential task of parenthood today.

The *TV On/Off Project* can become a new way of life for your family. Here are some of the rewards that lie ahead:

• Family involvement in *TV On/Off* can draw everyone closer. Just working through a mutual commitment to improve your lives can strengthen family ties. Granted, the going may be rough at times, but everyone will be suffering together. The *Project* can be an important family venture, with everyone contributing their share to make it work.
• A subtle kind of reassessment of family values will occur in this process of improving individual and family use of TV. As you talk about personal reactions to TV, as you make decisions on how to use leisure time, as you discover other interests, you will be experimenting with large-scale changes in habits and improvements in behavior. For children especially, many newly formed attitudes and self-discoveries will become lifelong assets. In innumerable ways, children's development can benefit from new interests and hobbies, acquired skills, broadened knowledge, and, best of all, new enthusiasms. It is not too much to imagine that each of you can enrich your lives by this experience.
• Some of the distortions of life shown on TV can be handled through your efforts to analyze what is seen and heard; as a result, your family will begin to use the medium more selectively. This process will help everyone

develop powers of discrimination through which they can filter away the effects of cruelty and inhumanity shown on the screen and substitute positive, healthy ideas.

- There is a strong possibility that some of the minor daily irritations in family coexistence, such as crankiness, squabbling, aggressiveness, nervousness, and noise will be lessened.
- There is an equally good chance that valuable qualities—such as cheerfulness and sociability—and worthwhile activities—such as reading, conversation, creative activities, imaginative play—will be increased.

The fact that the *TV On/Off Project* can lead to so many desirable changes in family life is a strong incentive to give it a try. Read on for practical suggestions about how to prepare yourself and your children for starting it.

TV On/Off

The Family in Our TV Society

Television has turned out to be one of the most phenomenal of all human inventions. It touches lives more intimately and pervasively than anything that predates it, with the possible exception of the discovery of fire. Not even the printing press or the automobile have had such a powerful effect on so many. Wherever it has become available, it has gradually changed people's habits and behavior to the extent that the generations who have grown up with TV differ significantly from their predecessors.

TV was greeted with wonder and pleasure when it was first introduced in the middle '40s and its popularity has swept across the nation. It has permeated to all but the most remote places. TV antennae dot every kind of home, from the urban highrise to the Indian reservation house. Use of television has evolved into a commonly shared life-style for the majority of Americans. Nowadays the family without a set is considered odd. In most strata of society a person is expected to be knowledgeable about TV fare. Among children it is absolutely *de rigueur* to watch it. Those relatively few who come from setless homes contrive to grab every possible chance to see it elsewhere despite their parents' disapproval of it. TV is a new kind of status symbol, available to everyone. In the past there has been nothing comparable to it. Now, no matter on which side of the tracks children live, they can gain stature if they have stayed up the latest and seen the sensational "in" program. For many children, television serves as a social wedge of extreme importance!

Considered primarily as entertainment, television has become a kind of Pied Piper, continually luring everyone on a temporary escape from here and now. These "trips" are irresistible for most people, children especially. Once exposed to TV, they usually choose it as their preferred way to spend free time. Customary childhood pastimes are either cut down or never tried. Amazing as it may seem, today there are children of every age who rarely play together (although they may watch their favorite programs side by side); do not indulge in vigorous outdoor play; infrequently if ever read; seldom use their imaginations beyond the edges of TV-imposed ideas; and have scarcely tried to do anything creative on their own. The tragic part of this is that they are not aware of what they are missing, nor do their parents always realize the significance of these lost opportunities.

Television's role in our lives is even bigger than that of recreation. It is also a combined time thief and con artist. It is always there, ready to dangle its fascinating wares in front of us as replacement for more traditional ways to spend our leisure hours. We choose it almost unequivocally, overlooking how dull and pointless it often is when compared to the satisfaction of actively doing something ourselves. Inexperienced children are truly babes in the woods about this aspect of TV. They do not consider that it takes anything away from them. They consider it a nonstop Santa Claus whose bag of goodies is bottomless.

Television's teaching impact is felt by young and old alike and is of great significance in all our lives. It beams an unending stream of information at us. For better or for worse, it fills our heads with ideas, facts, rumors, misinformation, biases, irrelevancies, someone else's hidden agendas, useful and useless suggestions about what to buy, and propaganda of all kinds. As one of our children's teachers, TV is unquestionably skillful in communicating its messages to them, directly or insidiously. Although loath to admit this, we are beginning to see that TV has usurped some of our prerogatives in the guidance of our children.

Television is becoming suspect as the perpetrator of many of the social problems with which we are now confronted. Although other innovations in this never static twentieth century can also share some of the responsibility for the alterations in human behavior, it must be admitted that TV may be a primary source of these. It has become such a widespread, time-consuming, and common habit that it is bound to affect us. We ingest it daily as we do food. Such psychosocial influences on us were either less powerful or nonexistent before the TV age. The main dilemmas it raises are that no one is sure how harmful an intruder it is nor what to do about breaking its spell. Television is deeply entrenched in our lives; it cannot be easily eliminated.

If you contrast childhood today with your own (or your parents' childhoods if you grew up with TV), you will discover some important behavioral changes. Looking for these is intriguing; turn yourselves into anthropologists to study the customs of people (your children!) different from yourselves. It is always wise to be aware that the environment in which your children live, even though you are a part of it, is not the same *in their eyes* as you believe it to be. Adults are too conditioned by their own life experiences to have reactions similar to children's. Adopt the scientist's professionalism of objectivity as you think back about what childhood used to be and what it is now. The contrasts can help you see more clearly both the good and bad effects TV has on your family life and on your children.

Below is the first of many things you can try in order to raise your consciousness, sharpen your sensitivities, soul-search, or just get in closer touch with your own feelings and opinions on a variety of subjects. The purpose of Awareness Activities is to help you become involved in the *Project* in a more personal and hopefully more satisfying way.

AWARENESS ACTIVITY

Look Back

Pause for a minute to recollect what you did with your free time when you were young, approximately the same age as your children. This is an important exercise at this very moment, to turn back the pages of your own history so that you can research what interested you as a child. What were your favorite pastimes? What did some of the children you knew do? What were the popular games, toys, books, activities then?

Next, while you are still reacting to the memories and feelings just called up from your childhood, take a broad jump from one extreme to another. Travel the distance from your *then* to your children's *now*. Think about some of the main differences in the two times.

Your findings from Look Back will depend on where and when you grew up. Despite variations, however, most people recall some commonalities to childhood in the past that differ from that of contemporary children. The following list includes those contrasts most frequently mentioned. *Before TV,* children:

- played together more often
- played outdoors more
- played more traditional games, like marbles, jacks, etc.
- spent more time being inventive and creative
- were interested in more "hands-on" activities such as arts and crafts, building club houses, etc.
- explored their neighborhoods more
- formed their own clubs or teams
- were given more freedom to go places alone (the world was relatively safer then)

- helped at home more
- had more homework
- read more
- seemed to be more polite and considerate
- seemed to respect their elders more
- were more interested in family gatherings, outings, celebrations of holidays
- were more naive
- seemed less troubled

Children today bear the marks of TV's touch. They differ from before-TV children in many mixed-up ways. They know more about a variety of things, but many of them cannot read. They can remember months-old advertising slogans, but many cannot recall after a few hours what they were taught in school. They can sit for hours in front of the TV screen but have no patience to sit quietly at the dinner table. The comparisons can go on, some acceptable, others distressing.

As part of your Look Back activity, think about parent-child relationships. *Before TV,* parents and children:

- spent more time together
- talked together more
- shared more joint projects and chores
- ate more meals together
- went together to visit relatives and family friends more often, and received more visits from them
- did not ordinarily discuss subjects such as sex, violence, death, social diseases, etc.

Parental behavior has also undergone some changes in the last few decades. In comparison to the past, parents today tend to be:

- more permissive
- less demanding
- less domineering
- more democratic
- more conciliatory
- somewhat less involved in terms of time spent together
- less patient
- less consistent

Not all changes in parent behavior are due to television, of course, but TV's potential to influence must be taken into account. Nor can its importance as a tool in the power struggle between parents and children be overlooked. TV has been used by parents to bribe, punish, bargain, reward, pacify, distract, bide time, baby-sit, and on and on.

It is pointless to condemn parents for many of the things they do. They are the innocent and often unwilling victims of cultural attitudes and habits. In this era of rapid social shifts, it has become progressively more difficult to recognize, understand, and cope with constant waves of change. Many of parents' motivations in deliberately using television with their children are well-intentioned. First of all, they believe there are useful things their children can learn from it. TV as education has been strongly touted, especially for preschool children. It is only natural that parents view it as a form of education, and allow their children to use it in the hope that they will benefit from it. Frequently, watching TV is seen as the lesser of two evils, and is chosen as being a safer thing for children to do than is playing outside, where danger lurks, or getting into some mischief if left to their own devices. As a distraction and as a companion to an upset or sick child, TV has no equal, if parents have limited time to devote to that child.

The *TV On/Off Project* does require a commitment of time and effort. Some of the suggested activities require more than others. For some parents, there just is not enough time for all of these. Individual use of time will have to be on a trial-and-error basis. Fortunately, there are many shortcuts you can take. Occasionally you may find that squeezing out a few extra minutes from your busy schedule brings an immediate payoff. Just witnessing your family's enthusiastic participation in an activity that frees it momentarily from TV's hold can be a rich reward!

One way to find time is to plan it more carefully. If you take a close overview of how you spend a week's worth of time, you may find a place here and there when you can cut down on something temporarily to devote time to the *Project*.

Another way to solve the too-little-time problem is to solicit others' help for the preparation of some of the suggested Helpful Things to Do. Perhaps nonworking or retired friends would be willing to lend their hands, talents, and ideas. Older children in the family or neighorhood can also be helpful. One can never tell when such a request would be considered flattering and a pleasure to the person asked. An added benefit of this can be that the more people who know about and are active in the *Project*, the more interesting it will become for everyone involved.

Now is the appropriate moment to introduce the first Helpful Thing to Do. Helpful Things to Do are activities to try with the family. They are varied, running the gamut from the kind of activities described below, to analyzing difficult situations, to just enjoying yourselves. Their purpose is to help your children make better use of the TV they watch, or find alternative activities to interest them.

The following Helpful Things to Do are intended to enrich some of the family customs that cement its members together and, at the same time, to serve as distractions from television.

HELPFUL THINGS TO DO

Family History

The purpose of this activity is to reinforce family solidarity.

- Go over baby books, photo albums, heirlooms.
- Talk about important past happenings in the family, including information about grandparents, aunts, uncles, ancestors, everyone.
- Plan a family gathering, inviting near and far distant relatives.
- Encourage your children to start correspondences with out-of-town cousins.

Family Customs Mix

Your children will enjoy some of the things you liked when you were young.

- Ask your parents or older relatives about some of the family's customs that are no longer followed. Try to start some of these again. Mix them with the customs you have established in your own family.
- Have a relatives' potluck party, asking everyone to bring some kind of food they especially liked in their childhood.
- Plan an heirloom-display day. Ask each relative to bring some treasure from the family's past.

Visit The Old Country

The rediscovery of where your ancestors lived can be fascinating. It will give your family a new awareness of your roots.

- Use maps to identify the places your ancestors came from originally.
- Find out as much as you can about those places, as they were and what they are like today.
- If any known relatives still live there, start correspondences with them. Exchange photos.
- Try to visit them and ask them to visit you.
- Try to find out if there are any local clubs of people of your ancestors' nationality. Ask to attend their meetings to learn more about their customs.

Let's Start

It is never too late to begin new family customs.

- Pool family suggestions for something interesting and fun that the family can do together.
- Select one of the ideas to carry out immediately.
- Plan to include the others later on.
- Turn the new customs you like best into family traditions; repeat them on a regular basis.

Language Brush-Up

- Make a family project of learning some simple phrases in the language(s) in your background. You can find books, records, or cassettes to help you with this.
- If your ancestors came from England, Scotland, Ireland, or Wales, read samples of those countries' old literature. See how much you can understand.
- Use some simple "old country" phrases in the family as a kind of private language.

Concentration on family history and traditions adds to children's understanding of how people act, giving them a broader background of information to compare with television versions. The more aware they are of their own family uniqueness, the more discerning they can be of others' behavior.

Restoring a sense of family is an important part of the *TV On/Off Project*. Stretch your imagination to envision the TV set as another member of the family with whom you must contend. It intrudes itself into your home with its bag of visual and audio tricks. These carry much more weight in family life than we like to admit. What TV offers can often take precedence over everything else at the moment. A program popular with the family can regulate meal hours and other aspects of the daily schedule. Attempts to talk to people who are watching TV are often futile or nonrewarding. In these and other ways, the TV set does raise a barrier to family communications and togetherness. The following chapters suggest ways to cut down on TV's intrusion, as well as ways to make TV serve as a bridge to more communication with the family.

TV -
A Personal Habit

Television may be the most effective binder of all the mass media in that it reaches so many people simultaneously. It becomes something we all have in common, providing everyone with more or less identical information and entertainment. TV, the leveler of all people! TV, the important Town Crier!

Despite its ability to meld people together, however, television affects us all differently. As viewers we each carry our unique psychological bag with us. Within that bag is an *at this moment* mixture of inner selves: our feelings, attitudes, assumptions, anxieties, unfulfilled wishes, and vulnerabilities, for starts. Television viewing is a private, personal affair!

Before parents make any attempt to change family viewing habits, therefore, it is essential to understand the impact of television on each member of the family. The activities in this chapter provide ways to collect and evaluate detailed information about the effects of TV on each individual. As you focus on viewing habits, many questions will undoubtedly surface. Some of these you may have mulled over before; for example, the following are those most commonly raised by parents and teachers:

Are children (or adults) watching TV too much?
Are they seeing the wrong kind of programs?
Are they becoming tense or anxious as a result of what they watch?
Are they learning questionable values?

The activities described below will give you the information you need to answer such crucial questions and to help your family understand what changes in TV habits may be needed.

Begin by considering the role TV plays in your own life. Complete the following Prequestionnaire for an overview of your own use of and reactions to TV.

AWARENESS ACTIVITY

Prequestionnaire

Personal Use of and Reactions to TV

Date: _____ My free hours per day:
How my free hours are spent:
How much approximate time I spend per day watching TV:
My favorite programs:
My favorite personality on TV:
How do I feel about TV?
Does TV help me relax? If so, how and when?
Does TV add pressures to my life? If so, how?

Next, ask other members of the family to also take the Prequestionnaire. If you make it a family happening, with everyone doing it at once, it may seem less awesome. After everyone has finished, talking about each person's answers will possibly give some new information that will be useful in helping you decide what next to do. You will undoubtedly gain insights into yourselves as a result of this process. Such a family gathering can set the tone for the joint efforts to follow on the shared *Project* you are starting. It can be an enjoyable experience. Focusing on this shared interest can also prove to be a unifying force.

It is important to require that everyone fill out the questionnaire in writing. This allows everyone to save the answers for comparison later on with those of a *Project* Postquestionnaire. In addition, writing the answers to a questionnaire forces people to concentrate more thoroughly in their attempts to clarify their thoughts.

The questionnaires are useful for everyone, even those too young to write. It is best to allow enough time for them to talk about their reactions to the questions in detail, starting with favorite programs. For very young children, it may be necessary to reword some of the questions so that they will understand them better. Patient waiting for the children to state their comments is vital here. The interviewer should be careful not to put words in the children's mouths or make assumptions about what they think. Their own reactions will be the most appropriate for future planning.

In addition to the questionnaire, there are other steps you can take to help decide what individual goals to set with each family member. In order to accomplish this in the fairest, least arbitrary way, it is best to continue to use as scientific an approach as possible. You can combine several methods here that should give a clear picture of individual habits and behavior.

HELPFUL THINGS TO DO

Weekly Time Chart

The first thing to do is to make a Weekly Time Chart for each family member. A chart like this reveals the state of TV habits at one glance. It is a factual document too, about which there can be little or no argu-

Week of May 8   Debbie's Weekly Time Chart

Total TV = 17 hrs.

Time	Mon.	Tues.	Wed.	Thurs.	Fri.	Sat.	Sun.
7-9	dressed ate, etc.	D.A. TV=½ hr.	D+A	D.A. TV=½hr		ate TV	up late
9-11	school		TV in school ½ hr			TV 2 hrs.	Sunday School
11-1							TV = ½ hr
1-3						to beach	at Nana's TV= 1 hr
3-5	played TV=½hr.	helped Mom.	Scouts	played	over at Janet's		played outside
5-7	TV=1hr. supper	TV = ½ hr	TV= ½ hr.	TV= ½ hr	TV = ½ hr.		TV = 2 hrs.
7-9	TV= 1½ hrs.	home-work	TV = 1 hr.	home-work	TV = 8:00	TV = 8:00	
Extra Hours Up					to 10:00	to 10:30	

Sample Weekly Time Chart

ment. Such a chart can prove to be a valuable tool to use for convincing and reminding one another of why TV habits need to be changed.

The use of red pencil or crayon to mark the times TV is watched makes the chart easier to read.

The best procedure with these charts is to ask the children to help make them and fill them in. Older children can be encouraged to create their own versions, plain or elaborate. The main guidance parents might offer is an occasional reminder to be sure the children are keeping their charts up-to-date. For the preschoolers, parents or older children in the family will have to make and fill in charts, but always with the younger children alongside. Unless you get the children in on the act, the charts will not be as meaningful to them. It is a good idea to post the charts in a prominent spot.

To get the most accurate accounting of how each child spends time on a daily basis, at least three or four week's worth of duplicate charts can be made, with carbon paper or by photocopying, to be filled in on consecutive weeks, or every other week for an extended six-to eight-week period. With those children whose routine varies little from week to week, a one- or two-week survey will probably be enough.

The charts are significant for several reasons. Most important, they serve as an introduction to the *TV Off* part of the *Project* (Chapters 3 and 4). Through the charts you can get each child immediately involved. Also they will be literal indicators of everyone's daily activities. You can read and discuss each chart individually so that together you can decide if TV is taking too much time out of a person's day or week.

HELPFUL THINGS TO DO

What We Watched Chart

What We Watched is another type of chart that helps pinpoint family TV customs. On this chart, everyone's viewing is to be recorded.

It is essential to have an accounting of what and how much you grown-ups use TV too, for a variety of reasons. Including yourselves in the *Project* shows your sincerity and your willingness to share in more than just the decisions and guidance. By charting yourselves, you also set a good example for your children to follow, almost an incentive to them. Such democratic participation will be more effective in guaranteeing your children's cooperation than will a one-sided, autocratic approach. And you do stand to learn things about yourselves and TV by a more studied view of your own behavior. Being an adult does not necessarily eliminate the possibility that you are not using the medium to your best personal advantage. Children are

M = Mom J = Jerry	Programs and Who Watched Week of 5/8	D = Dad C = Carol
Mon	News-D Capt. Kan.-C	Dinah- M,J,C Mary T. Moore -J&C Elec. Co.- J&C	6p.m. News-D Family Feud-D,J,C C.Burnett-D,M,J,C	9 p.m. Movie - D & M
Tues	Capt. Kan.-C	Cartoons-J&C The Monkees- C&J	News -D Muppets-M,J,C Film-D&J	Laverne -M,D,J 3's Co.-M,D,J Carter Co.- D News- D
Wed	News-D Capt. Kan.-C	Cartoons- J&C	I Love Lucy -J,C Newlywed- J, C	News -D
Thurs	Capt. Kan.-C	Dinah-M&C Leave it to Beaver-C	News -D THe FBI-D,J,C Kotter-D&J	Movie -D,M News -D
Fri	Capt. Kan.-C	Flintstones-C Cartoons-C&J Sesame St.-C	Flintstones Game-D,J +C Tabitha -D,J&C	Movie -D,M News-D
Sat	Car- toons- C & J	Sports - D&J Sports-J	Game -D, M,J,C Bob Newhart,-J&C Rookies J&C	
Sun	Car- toons C&J		All in the Family - M, D& J	Movie -D News-D

Sample What We Watched Chart

not the only ones who waste time in front of a set, or who are badly affected by some of what they see, or who become addicted!

Along with these exploratory charts that provide a clear picture of how often and what programs the family watches, there is another kind of observation that can be important. This concerns people's outward reactions to TV viewing. What it requires is a kind of ongoing watchfulness of what seems to be happening to your children and yourselves as a result of TV. Ordinarily, writing all this down might seem excessively time consuming. However, for those children who are likely to strongly resist your efforts to help them make some changes, it might be worthwhile to write a spot-check record of what they do in front of the TV set to use as convincing proof that all is not well. Or, better still, a discussion to point out some of their reactions immediately after you have observed them can help. Children often are not aware of how different they are when under TV's influence.

AWARENESS ACTIVITY

Take A Close Look

It is important to observe the same person at different times in order to get a broad perspective of his or her responses to a variety of programs.

Listed below are the many kinds of behavior to note:

- physical behavior:
    position—prone; seated; slouched
    posture—relaxed; stiff
    body movements—still; twitching; restless
    hand—still; moving—what doing?
    facial and eye expressions
- verbal behavior:
    conversation and/or any spoken reactions
    accompanying noises
    laughter; shouting; singing; sighing; gasping
- overall behavior:
    absorbed
    acts out what is happening on screen
    intermittent attention
    easily distracted
    doing something else at same time
    turns back to or leaves set

- moods before, during, and after:
  relaxed
  tense, irritable
  happy
  glum, sad
  not noticeably changed
- why set was turned off:
  program over
  something else to do
  interruption
  boredom
  fatigue
- approximate time spent at set
- time of day
- voluntary discussion of program(s) just seen

In order to gain a truer picture of TV-affected conduct, it is a good idea to become more alert to a child's or your own behavior in other routine situations, such as at meals, with friends, and so forth. There may or may not be differences in your actions when watching TV and at other times, but if there are it can be of significance. TV can produce hangovers of many kinds and intensities! What is seen and heard can cause subtle emotional variations, often without a person's total awareness. These emotional shifts seep out in response to the people and the situations encountered after TV watching.

HELPFUL THINGS TO DO

TV Freaks

This a fun way for people to show their impressions of TV's effect on themselves and each other. It can be played from several different angles: when TV is on; during a specific show; when TV is turned off; if TV is denied; if TV is interrupted; after a controversial program; after a person has been watching a long time; after scary, silly, funny, educational shows; and so on. There are two versions:

Face Drawings.   Draw half faces of each family member. Use carbon paper to make duplicate copies. Ask each person to complete the drawings. Talk about them afterwards.
Charades.   Ask people to act out their impressions one at a time, then talk about them afterwards.

Draw first

Fill in later

Sample Face Drawings

Flip Book

This is a more lasting, less personalized adaptation of TV Freaks.

- Use sheets of heavy construction paper or light cardboard.
- Draw as many different faces with a variety of facial expressions as you can, on one side of the page only.
- Punch three equidistant holes (or adjust to loose-leaf notebook holes) in each page.
- Cut pictures into three sections.
- Put in a notebook or tie together with string.
- To use, flip for different facial combinations. Discuss how these symbolize people's reactions to TV.

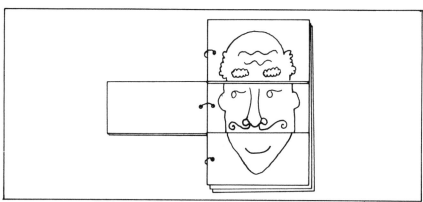

Sample Flip Book

Once you have a clear picture of your family's use of TV and of the effects of TV on moods and behavior, it is time to consider the meaning of television as an important factor in each person's life.

AWARENESS ACTIVITY

In-House TV Popularity Rating

Ask yourselves, individually or as a group, the following questions to determine TV's importance in your family. If the answers are written they may reflect more careful thought.

- List ten of your favorite things to do, in order of importance.
- If you had to give up half of these, which would you want to keep? List in order of importance.
- What if you could only watch half of your usual TV programs? Which would you give up? Why?
- What would you do if TV were abolished from your home?
- Do you consider that TV is important to you? If so, in what way and why?

In a lighter vein, you can ask yourselves the following questions:

- If you could receive anything as a gift provided you gave away your TV set, what would you select?
- If your TV set was sold, what gifts (tangible and otherwise) would you each give other family members for consolation and/or replacement?

HELPFUL THINGS TO DO

TV-Side Chats

Bring your family together to pool their thoughts and feelings about what TV means in your life. You may wish to share your answers to the In-House TV Popularity Rating. Listed below are some additional topics for family discussion. The best times for such talks are after everyone has been viewing together. It is a good idea to hold TV-Side Chats regularly.

Suggested Topics

TV as:

luxury	pleasure	source of learning
necessity	pain	vicarious experience
social imperative	recreation	time filler
companion	escape	"in" thing to do
substitute for reading		

At this point you have a considerable amount of information regarding the role TV plays in each person's life. Evaluation of that information will help you decide what changes need to be made.

A basic issue is whether family members overuse television. A criterion of overuse of television is hard to define because there are so many variables involved in how and why each one of us uses TV, and what it does to and for us. However, even though it is risky to state that over two hours of average daily viewing is too much, let's use that amount of time as our measuring stick. Current statistics show that sets in American homes are on for an average of six hours per day, so our two hour maximum may seem unreasonably low. In light of the potential harm of excessive and long-term use of TV that researchers' warnings reveal, however, it might be smart to opt for the premise: less TV is better!

It is often tricky, too, to determine whether or not individual children's television viewing habits need changing. Even those who watch moderately or spasmodically may show questionable behavior in front of the set, or as a result of TV. To help you diagnose your own children, here are some general characteristics of appropriate TV use for comparison:

an hour or less of daily viewing
careful program selection
ability to forego watching if interrupted
low priority to TV on list of preferred ways to use leisure time
willingness to turn off questionable programs
interest in screening new shows, especially those recommended by parents
habit of discussing everything seen with parents
interest in further "researching" new things learned on TV
ability to intersperse active play (preferably outdoors) with use of TV
elimination of TV as something to do with friends
use of books and other reading materials as a source of recreation

The criteria outlined above require a great deal of maturity on the part of most children. Realistically, one cannot expect such responsible behavior much before the average child is at least seven or eight. Under parental supervision, however, provided it is not heavy-handed, children *can be guided* towards more sensible viewing habits.

To make a more studied evaluation of whether or not members of your family are watching too much television, refer again to the Weekly Time and What We Watched charts; then ask yourself the following questions about each person:

- What percentage of free time is spent at TV?
- When alternative activities are available? How often does the person select them instead of TV?
- Does that person generally do no, a few, or many other things as well as watch TV?

If TV seems to be the main pastime, it may be overused. If it excludes other activities usually considered normal behavior for that individual's age range, such as active play for children and avocations or hobbies for adults, overuse is again indicated.

Many parents conclude that their children (and often they themselves) would benefit by watching less TV. But turning off the television set is a step that most people regard as most difficult. The next two chapters explain how you and your family can change your TV habits.

Recommendation: Some TV Turn Off

If you have determined that your family needs to change its TV viewing habits by eliminating certain programs or cutting down on TV watching, it is time to launch the *TV Off* part of the *Project*. A word of caution is appropriate here. The more facts you have about your family's TV watching habits, the stronger your case becomes for changing the family's viewing customs. So in the collection of information described in the previous chapter, patience is the magic word! In the long run, your efforts will be more effective if you have devoted a fairly long time to the preliminary step of analyzing viewing habits than if you act quickly, only partially armed by persuasive evidence.

If you feel confident that you have done enough research on family viewing habits, the next step is to prepare yourself to discuss the *TV Off Project* with your family. Your chances of success will be greater if you are psychologically prepared for your children's reactions to *TV Off*. Below is an Awareness Activity for all the adults in the family, as well as for those who frequently are in and out of the house.

AWARENESS ACTIVITY

On Trying to Give Up Something We Enjoy

Think of something you do ordinarily that has become a valued habit, such as:

watching TV	talking on the phone
reading	visiting friends
walking	listening to music

How would you feel if you were asked to give this up partially or entirely?

- How would you accept this restriction?
- How would you feel towards people who had ordered it?
- How do you suppose you might react at the time you want to do it and are not allowed?
- What do you think you might do instead?
- How would you handle your feelings of loss?
- What would you try to do about it over the long run?
- Do you imagine that over a period of time you could get used to doing without it?

HELPFUL THINGS TO DO

Rehearsal Role Playing

Sometimes it helps to rehearse ahead of time anticipated difficult encounters. As the *TV Off Project* is more apt to be resisted than welcomed enthusiastically by most children, as well as by some addicted adults, it may be a good idea to playact scenes beforehand. This can be done in your heads or more effectively in front of a mirror, speaking out loud. For realism, you can even role play the other family members as well as yourselves, entering into an imaginary dialogue. This may aid you in your thinking and actually unearth useful ideas you can take advantage of later on. This type of preparation gives you experience that may serve you well when you need it most! Suggested scenes to playact in advance:

- The children argue that they do not watch too much TV, but you are convinced they do.
- The other parent is not sold on the need for the *Project*.
- A child interprets the *Project* as undeserved punishment.
- Children gang up and say that the *Project* is dumb and that nobody else they know has to do such a thing.

When you have prepared yourself to deal with the reactions of your children, you are ready to call a family conference for the family's study of the information you have gathered and for collective decisions about what you ought to do.

Such conferences as these deserve a special time and setting. They are far too important to be done casually. For this reason it might be wise to settle on a time most convenient for the entire family to get together. Plans to serve the family's favorite snack then never hurts. Refreshments have an amazingly good effect on people when they are working hard on something difficult.

Although it may seem strange at first to establish ground rules for a family conference, in this case it is advisable. Because this *Project* is a serious one involving everyone, a more formal approach will put it in proper perspective. The rules themselves can be set in as democratic a way as possible. The more everyone has an opportunity to help make them, the more apt they are to follow them. In general terms, rules might include:

willingness to listen to everyone's ideas and opinions
willingness to hear everyone out, without unnecessary interruptions and/or judgments
real efforts *not* to argue
good sportsmanship

Centering the family discussion on TeeVeeitis (too much TV viewing) cures helps set the stage. To set a good example and perhaps ease the way for the children, it helps to focus the opening discussion on one or both parents. If you kept charts on yourself, you should refer to them to help you decide what changes you plan to make in your own viewing. You should report also on whatever Awareness Activity Take a Close Look has revealed to you about yourselves. Others will become more sensitive to their own reactions if you share such revelations as "I never realized before how jumpy I am after I watch _____" or "I discovered I don't really enjoy _____; it makes me feel depressed. I am not going to watch it anymore."

It never hurts to restate your reasons for the *TV Off Project.* Now as you involve your entire families, you want to be ready to convince them of the necessity for it. It may require a great deal of talking, especially with those children who use TV the most. They will be hard to reach. Adapt the sales pitch that seems best for your specific family. There are several general approaches, however, that can be used as starters:

- Encourage members of the family to tell if and why they believe this *Project* is necessary.
- After everyone has spoken, you can give any additional information or ideas you have. In some instances it may be necessary to scare the children by emphasizing the known bad effects of excessive TV viewing.

- Compare the importance of the *TV Off Project* to other familiar preventive care, such as having one's eyes and teeth examined and treated regularly, or putting braces on teeth to improve mouth formations. You can mention that splints and casts are used to reset broken bones, and that the *Project* will help accomplish a similar healing process for the illness called TeeVeeitus.
- You can express your optimism that family members will cooperate on the *Project,* and that it will prove worthwhile for everyone. Ideally your belief in its effectiveness will be caught by the rest of the family and will act as a motivating force.
- You can make clear from the beginning that you grown-ups want to be as helpful as possible. A part of this will be to explain that you know the *TV Off Project's* demands may often seem difficult, but that you will always try to be flexible and open to suggestions. At the outset you would do well to try to impress on your children that you will try not to be domineering or overdemanding *Project* directors.
- It never hurts to keep reminding everyone that the *Project* is a family affair, that grown-ups and children are in it together working for each other's benefits.

To begin setting specific goals with your children, consult their Weekly Time and What We Watched charts once more. These will provide information needed to decide how much less time to watch and what program(s) to eliminate. As always, plan for this on an individual basis. The best chances for success require a careful fit, somewhat like being measured for a pair of shoes. As with shoes, consideration also has be to given to style—what does the person like best, and what is most appropriate for his or her needs?

Encourage your children to make their own decisions of what to give up, unless you have strong reasons for thinking that a specific show is inappropriate. Explain why that one is no longer acceptable. If your advice is sought on what shows might be given up, help the child reach a decision by talking over these points:

- Which programs are liked best, least; which ones fit in the middle category?
- Compare programs with each other in terms of how often and during what hours they are screened. Omit ones that conflict with time that could be spent playing, helping around the house, and so forth.
- If the child has a problem deciding, suggest compromises, such as eliminating one show per week of a series that is shown several times, or watching a one-time-per-week show every other week.

Discuss reward systems in detail and draw up verbal or written contracts in advance (see the activities described below). Here are a few cautionary suggestions:

- Plan on small *TV turn-offs* at first, with gradual increases as each person becomes accustomed to them.
- Be flexible. Minor changes may be required, particularly in the beginning steps.
- Maintain a light, humorous touch as much as possible.
- Praise and encourage all attempts at cooperation.

Even if your family agrees that the *Project* is not a bad idea, everyone's main interest probably will be centered on the here-and-now payoff. As it may be difficult to convince some people, children especially, of the long-range benefits, immediate rewards will be necessary. A good idea is to ask family members what they think might be interesting rewards. Some of their ideas may be amazingly easy to fulfill. You can pool their suggestions and then add your own in order to reach workable compromises. When plans for each person are settled, an individually selected reward can be included.

In most instances, the best rewards are *not* money, sweets, or purchased things. As incentives you can offer privileges, such as staying up later (not to see TV, however!); favorite family pastimes, such as picnics; or, best of all, more of your own time devoted to one person at a time. Sometimes such prizes are the most valued.

The younger the children, the more accepting they will be of simple rewards. Probably they will be really excited about the prospect of a picnic or the chance to spend time alone with one or both parents. The more you can match their enthusiasm with your own, the better the results will be. If you have difficulty occasionally with this, you might do well to picture your family a few years into the future watching more rather than less TV! That ought to help raise your fervor to the proper pitch.

More concessions may have to be reached with older children. Whatever works with them is probably the wisest way to go, within reason. If their payoff boils down to money, perhaps the best handling of that is to set up a savings account (a real one in a bank or an I.O.U. system) towards the purchase of something big. A new bicycle, a sleeping bag, or a typewriter may prove to be a better motivation than small amounts of cash doled out on a weekly basis.

Actual tokens and/or time scorekeepers do wonders to keep people actively involved in the difficult task of *TV turn-off*. They serve several purposes. At first they will be something new and different, and may especially intrigue the younger children, who probably will enjoy making or helping to make them. This will seem like a fringe benefit to the *Project* and may alleviate some of its sting. Tokens and scorekeepers will also be tangible evidence of the progress being made toward future rewards!

HELPFUL THINGS TO DO

Tokens

Tokens can be made of any kind of paper or thin cardboard, in any size or shape. The use of colored paper, crayons, or felt markers to show different amounts of time when TV is *not* watched makes their worth easily recognizable. For instance, yellow could equal fifteen minutes of *turn off;* pink, thirty minutes; green, forty-five minutes; white, one hour. Rewards can be decided on in advance for total *turn-off* time each week.

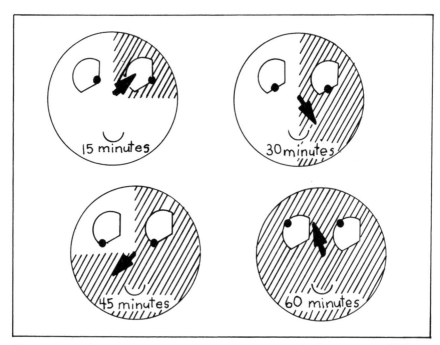

Reward Tokens For NOT Watching TV

Token Treasure Chest

A box ornately decorated (preferably by the child) can be used to hold different colored toothpicks, pieces of yarn, buttons, elastic bands, etc., each color or object representing the amount of *TV turn-off* time to be added up weekly for a reward, as above.

Token Tree

A many-branched tree can be drawn. Token color-coded leaves can either be crayoned on or cut out of colored paper and pinned on. The latter may be better as they are reusable.

A three-dimensional tree can be made out of a wire clothes hanger and mounted in a plastic container between crumpled wads of heavy paper or small stones so that it does not tilt as leaves are added. The color-coded leaves can be made of anything and attached with paper clips, bits of pipe cleaners, or string.

Turn-Off Thermometer

An enlarged drawing of an outdoor thermometer can serve as a weekly progress gauge. The markings should be for fifteen-minute intervals of *turn-off* time, to be colored in on a daily basis. Or, if preferred, a small movable arrow can be used to indicate *turn-off* times.

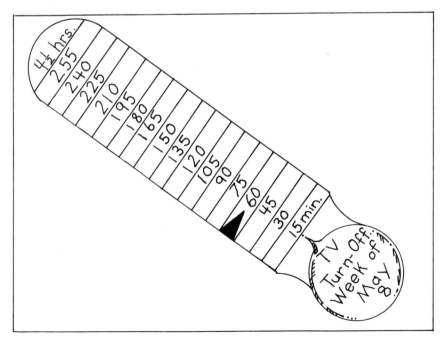

Sample Turn-Off Thermometer

Success Graph

A Success Graph shows fifteen-minute *turn-off* time segments extending from the bottom upwards on the left-hand margin from the graph. The bottom edge should be divided evenly into seven sections, one for each day of the week.

Individual Success Graphs can be made per person, or one graph can serve for the whole family by marking each individual's *turn-off* time in a different color.

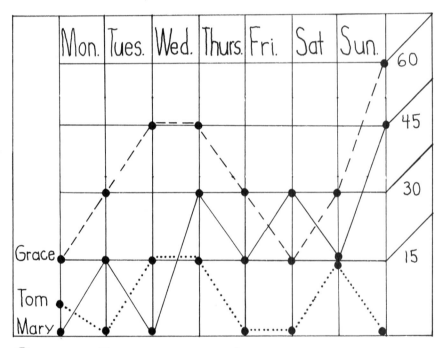

Sample Success Graph

Contracts

Contracts are formal agreements and actually may be preferred by older children (even adults may consider a form of written contract a necessary binder for their own use).

Each Contract can be drawn up after a careful planning of its goals and rewards.

For: _____   Date: _____

| Agreement |

I will try to:
A. Watch less TV
B. Cut down on viewing at least ½ hr. per day

| Reward |

For each ½ hr. less TV watched, I shall receive a token.
3 tokens = can stay later on playground Mon. & Wed.
6 tokens = family bike ride at beach.
10 tokens = can invite friend overnight.
Witnessed by: _____ Signed: _____

Sample TV Cut Down Contract

Miscellaneous Acknowledgments

In a spirit of family shared pride about people's progress, there are small ways of celebrating. Sometimes these add an air of festivity for successes achieved and with younger children are effective inducements for cooperation. At the same time they are diversions that might help to lighten the family atmosphere or temporarily interrupt grumblings about the *Project.*

Honor Hats, Paper Corsages or Boutonnieres. These can be simply made and awarded ceremoniously at supper to the person who has turned off TV for the longest period of time within the preceding twenty-four hours.

Merit Badges. Any kind of badge will do, the simpler the better, such as color-coded paper or yarn bows with the recipient's name on them. Collections of these can be kept in clear plastic jars, mounted on ribbon sashes, tied together to form a bouquet, or whatever makes them look most impressive. They should be prominently displayed as a constant reminder and inspiration that the *TV Off Project* is working.

Special Privilege of the Day.   A small privilege can be granted to the person with the best *TV turn-off* record of the preceding twenty-four hours. Young children might be pleased with such little honors as serving the dessert or choosing which story to be read at bedtime. An older child will probably like to have first chance at the bathroom or the comic page in the morning, or exclusive use of the phone for an afternoon. Special-privilege ideas are unlimited. All you have to do is consult your families for suggestions.

Once set in motion, the business of making and maintaining the various charts and rewards becomes less demanding and time consuming. Usually the children assume the bulk of the responsibility for them, particularly before the attraction of their newness wears away. By the time this happens, hopefully the family will be used to *TV Off* and will need fewer gadgets for motivation.

As your family practices *TV Off,* try the next activity. It is an effective way to indoctrinate very young children to the establishment of good TV habits. It can also help older children improve the way they use television.

TV VIEWER'S LICENSES
(For Very Young)

LEARNER'S PERMIT

FROM _____ TO _____

NOTE: Applicant must be accompanied by an adult when using television.

FOR: The Following Programs:_____

_____

TO PRACTICE:
* Spotting the difference between reality and make-believe.
* Talking about programs during and afterwards.

GRANTED TO: _____

TEMPORARY LICENSE   FROM _____ TO _____
FOR: Viewing (hours per day or week)

QUALIFICATION REQUIREMENTS:
Willingness to:
- Do homework and chores before turning on set.
- Play or be active before and after TV.
- Listen to parents' suggestions regarding use of TV.
- Call a parent if upset by anything seen on TV.
- Discuss programs afterwards with parent(s).

This Temporary License will be revoked if:
- Licensee watches more than allotted hours.
- Licensee gets poor grades in school.
- Licensee neglects chores and/or homework.
- Licensee becomes unusually irritable or moody.

GRANTED TO: _____

PERMANENT LICENSE   DATE _____
FOR: Maximum of _____ viewing hours per week.
Rotating right to choose program if use of set is in conflict.

QUALIFICATION REQUIREMENTS:
Willingness to:
- Consult with parents about program choices.
- Complete homework and chores before viewing.
- Play or be active before and after TV.
- Discuss programs afterwards with parent(s).
- Leave set when upset, frightened, or bored.
- Continue to be on the lookout for fiction versus fact.
- Do some reading or writing each day.

This License will be revoked if licensee:
- Watches more than allotted hours.
- Gets poor grades in school.
- Neglects chores and homework.
- Becomes unusually irritable or moody.

GRANTED TO: _____

The *TV Off* part of the *Project* is an important undertaking. If continued over a long enough period, it can produce gratifying results. In some families, improved behavior may ultimately be viewed as little short of a miracle: sunnier dispositions; more cooperation; more active play. Families in which children are still relatively young will find that the introduction of the *Project* now will almost guarantee that TV addiction and other questionable habits from which older children suffer will be avoided. The *Project* can serve as an immunization against a multitude of minor or major TV-related problems.

The next chapter offers further guidance for helping your family overcome addiction to the TV habit.

Winning the Battle Against TeeVeeitis

4

Although it may sound dramatic to suggest that you consider the way your family uses TV as a sickness, for some people it actually is. The problem is that this kind of sickness is hard to cure, mostly because its victims do not realize that anything is wrong. Perhaps the most important part of your preparation for the *Project* is your assumption that all is not well. Once you are convinced of that, you can play the "healer" role more effectively.

As you look more closely at your family's use of television, you may suspect that one or more members are close to addiction, or addicted. The main symptom of TV addiction is the inability to do without it. One classic example of this is the person on vacation away from home who prefers sitting in front of a TV to taking advantage of the available things to do at the vacation spot. There are innumerable variations of TV addicted behavior, of course. Even if you are not positive if anyone in your family is thus trapped by TV, take steps to counteract it notwithstanding. TV addiction is serious.

Treatment for addiction can be a slow process. It requires an inordinate amount of patience and perseverance for both the victim and the family. Your motivation has to remain on a high level. One way to achieve this is to make yourselves a few promises before you start. The most important of these is to never lose sight of your final goals, no matter how discouraged you may become. Constantly reevaluate what is occurring, and try not to become easily disheartened. Whenever people try to change customary habits by attempting something new, there is an element of chance involved. Complete success is not always in the cards. But it is worth the gamble. Remember, even a small amount of progress is better than none at all.

If you have read this far, chances are you are ready to commit yourself as completely as is reasonably possible to the *TV Off Project.* You look at your TV-riddled family and know you want to do whatever you can to cure them of their TV wounds. Such determination ought to keep you going. Your attitudes may run the gamut from "do or die" to "it's worth at least a try." The equation for success of any degree will depend on the amount of perseverance you invest.

HELPFUL THINGS TO DO

Pep Posters

It might be a good idea to make yourselves a few small reminder posters to tape on places where you frequently look, such as the bathroom mirror or refrigerator door. These messages may also be effective incentives to the rest of the family. Phrases such as these help:

WE CAN LICK THE MONSTER IN TV!
BETTER USE OF TV CAN GLUE THIS FAMILY TOGETHER.
TV CAN BE A FRIEND AND NOT A FOE.
LET'S TACKLE TV!

With your own motivation high, you are better prepared to help those in your family who may be victims of TV addiction. The fly in the ointment is that TV addicts, children particularly, do not understand why television is bad for them, or that they would be better off if they could kick the habit, at least somewhat. They resent interference, considering it an unfair and exaggerated infringement on their independence. Generally they fight hard against the cure. This type of resistance is on the conscious level; it is easy to recognize in their arguments, pleas, attempts to barter, and so forth.

More difficult to cope with are the pains of withdrawal. Over these children have virtually no control. Withdrawal can be compared to illness; how long it will last and how severe it will be is usually unpredictable. It is an attack on the entire eystem. It manifests itself in a variety of ways: irritability; extreme nervousness; moroseness; depression; apathy, appetite loss; excessive withdrawal into sleep.

As in any kind of weaning, there are several ways to handle TV addiction. They run the gamut from extreme measures to the application of large doses of tender loving care. You will have to experiment to find what works best for your patient(s). To cheer you on your way, I want to remind you that many people who have eliminated TV partially or completely from their lives have testified that they reaped many rewards they now consider immeasurably worth the struggle it entailed. Here are some suggestions for what to try.

HELPFUL THINGS TO DO

Withdrawal For Heavily Addicted Viewers

- Complete *TV Off*—The set is either: disconnected; turned to the wall; covered and used for knickknacks or, better still, books; given away or sold.
- Temporary *TV Off*—A designated period of no TV is preestablished, ranging from one week to several months.
- Partial *TV Off*—By family consensus the set is turned on for short periods only, either for one or two daily programs or for specials.
- Individual's *TV Off*—The amount of TV viewed is decided on an individual basis.

Aids To TV Withdrawal

Follow the preliminary suggestions given in Chapter 3, with the understanding that more handholding, and hence more of your time, will be required.
- If possible, try to initiate the person's first steps away from TV over a weekend or during vacation when activities different from the usual routine can be planned. No matter when, the easiest way to start is to get away from the house and the set; even a day away can help. Any change facilitates the process.
- Help compensate for the loss of TV by providing other activities. Chapters 10, 11, and 12 of this book suggest a multitude of specific projects. Here are some ideas to start with:

  - Go over the children's toys, books, records, etc. to ferret out seldom-used ones they might enjoy rediscovering.
  - Try to have on tap something new, time consuming, and entertaining, such as a large jigsaw puzzle, card games, a crossword puzzle book, jacks.
  - Arrange a children's corner in the kitchen or wherever you have to do your own work so that you can be close at hand.

- Consider different things the children can assume responsibility for that will be important services for the whole family's well-being and in which they can regularly participate. Such activities can include help with meal preparation; doing the laundry; reorganization of cupboards and closets; plant care. The purpose of such contributions is fourfold. It can build the children's commitment to the family, reinforce their own sense of competence, divert them from TV's lure, and take over some of your chores to free time for you to be with them!
- Offer the children a choice of things you can do together, such as read, go for a ride or walk, play, and so forth.
- Conjure up some ideas to suggest for unusual and/or fun things that the children can do on their own, such as take a bubble bath; listen to music; go on short walks or bike rides to "collect" different sights, smells, or sounds to report on after each trip (for example, ask the child to ride around the block and make note of all of the green things seen, or odors smelled, or sounds heard); follow written or picture clues prepared ahead of time by you for simple Treasure Hunts, with a small health snack or newly borrowed "surprise" library book for treasures.

Sample Treasure Hunt Clues

- Share information about the *Project* and what the children are doing with anyone else who spends time with them such as grandparents, other relatives, sitters, neighbors, teachers. The more these people reinforce the *Project* with the children, the easier it will be for all concerned.
- Try to compensate for the children's feelings of deprivation by being extremely considerate. Establish an open-forum situation in which the children can feel free to express their discontents and complaints to an attentive listener. If they can state these without threat of criticism or punishment, they will probably be less resentful of the whole affair. In order to encourage this emotional safety-valve, you can try the following:

  - Listen without moralizing, preaching, criticizing, or nagging.
  - Frequently repeat the long-range benefits of the *Project*.
  - Cling tightly to your own optimism.
  - Strive for calmness, objectivity, and consistency whenever possible.
  - Show understanding and empathy for the unpleasant aspects of the *Project* experienced by the family.
  - Share your own difficulties regarding the *Project* with emphasis on your dislike of having to impose it on everyone as well as your anger or guilt in having allowed TV to become too strong a family habit.

- Introduce humor whenever possible. One idea for this is to make Mood I.D. cards that can be kept at a handy spot available to

Sample Mood ID Cards

everyone. These small cards can be selected and pinned on by each person according to his or her emotional status of the moment. They serve as advance notices or warnings to others. The very act of choosing one or several to wear may also help put people in a better frame of mind.

- Remain firm about the rules you have set up. If you waver, you make it harder for the addict.
- Constantly praise whatever efforts are made and show your admiration for progress, no matter how small it may be. Tell others close to the family about what is going on and solicit their support for and cooperation with those involved, yourself included.
- Consult other people and resources for new and interesting ideas if you run out of things to do: ask the librarian, the child's teacher or youth group leader, the sitter, other children; look in magazines and books.
- Caution: remember that some children undergoing the cure may be sensitive about their friends' reactions. It might embarrass them to have other children find out. Respect your children's wishes for privacy if this is the case.
- Once the person seems cured, still maintain a careful watch on how he or she uses TV. Together set up a sensible TV "diet" that prevents chances for "readdiction."

The *TV Off Project* and treatment for addicted children are the hardest of all things required of parents in their guidance of family television use. Both cures are essential, however, and worth the serious attention they entail.

If you look at it another way, you can compare the *Project* to a high-interest-yielding Savings Account. Whatever effort you exert will go into your family's "life bank," to be cashed at some future time when the accrued assets will be very valuable. There is no threat of inflation with this account! What goes in now will be collectable at an immeasurably big increase no matter when the account is cashed.

Cutting down on the use of television is only one part of making better family use of TV. The next four chapters describe many ways of helping your family get the most out of the television they watch.

Put Heads Together in Front of the Set

5

○ ○ ○

However much we learn to limit our TV viewing, TV remains a large part of family life. The next step in the *TV On/Off Project* is to improve the family's use of television when the set is on.

The best approach you can take to help your family make better use of television is to watch with them. The more you do this, the more you will discover what a fantastic teaching tool TV is. As a matter of fact, its effectiveness as an avenue for learning poses many potential problems for parents and teachers, who often feel threatened by its influence. Children pick up such a large amount of information from TV that it is hard to know for sure what they have absorbed, either from direct messages or in a more subtle and covert way. Considering how completely and for how long television can hold children's attention, it must be admitted that TV rivals, if not outdistances, parents and teachers in influencing children's attitudes, opinions, and behavior. Herein lies the reason for making television a partner instead of an enemy in the guidance of children. Rather than permitting TV to abuse them, extract from it all the potential good it can add to your family life. Turn the "idiot box" into an idea-resource box!

Researchers' recommendations and common sense suggest that the best way for parents to help children benefit more from the television they see is to participate actively with every aspect of their use of it. An adult should be available to act as interpreter, guide, listener, buffer, motivating creative muse, provider of ideas, comforter, or whatever other kind of supporter the children require at the moment. For parents, the main difficulty concerns time. That is the tricky part—how to find enough time when children need it most. In the descriptions of activities involving parents and children, I have offered some suggestions for shortcuts and ways to make better use of time that you can adapt to fit your own responsibilities and schedules.

In order not to let the time element discourage you before you even begin, I want to emphasize that the most important ingredient you can give is your *continued interest* in your children's involvement with television. If it is impossible for you to do as much parallel viewing as you would like with the family, the habit of engaging the children in discussions after they have watched TV can be extremely effective. Actually, it is the sharing of their impressions and reactions that is of vital significance. The closer abreast you are to these, the better are your chances of remediation. Be assured, then, that any ways you find to supply your children with safety-valves after they have watched television can be almost as helpful as if you had been with them in front of the set.

There are, however, many advantages that result from parent-children parallel viewing. One is that shared viewing gives parents and childen a mutual interest. Another is that parents who watch with their children are in a better position to control how long children watch and what they see, and to introduce them to programs they have not yet tried. Furthermore, by observing children in front of the set, a parent can discover what is happening to them. Their reactions reveal a great deal about their level of comprehension and their feelings. With shared viewing, a parent can alleviate immediately any anxieties that may be stirred in children.

Another advantage is that through discussion with a parent, children gain a better understanding of what they are seeing. Family discussions about programs viewed together also become open sesames for airing and sharing important concepts, particularly about acceptable behavior and common-sense methods to solve problems.

Finally, TV lends itself to the development of many reading-readiness or reading-improvement skills that parents can encourage such as:

- the perception of audio and visual messages
- the analysis of the plot or main theme of a story
- the consideration of the sequence of events in a story
- the search for the meaning of a character's action or behavior
- the use of language and the practice of descriptive abilities
- the enlargement of a child's vocabulary

In shared viewing, a parent becomes a mediator between children and TV. Here are some specific suggestions that can make your role as mediator more successful:

- If you are not accustomed to watching television with the family, explain why you are interested in starting to do so. Among your reasons, you might include the fact that you want to find out more about what your children are watching and why they like their chosen programs.
- Start gradually, perhaps watching one program per day for about a week. The main reason for not jumping in full force is to allow a warm-up period for everyone involved. A good show to start with is the family's favorite.
- At first, remain a relatively passive TV companion. Rather than talking a lot yourself, use the time to listen to and to observe your children.
- Little by little, start to engage your children in short conversations while watching. Be forewarned that this may not work with everyone. Some people cannot talk during a program, being unable to handle the interruptions. If you find this to be the case with one or more of your children, don't make an issue of it. Just plan to talk immediately afterwards while the shows are still fresh in everyone's minds.
- During programs, brief comments work best. Here are some examples:

  - "Remember that!"—to pinpoint something you feel should be talked over later.
  - "Is that scary?" or "What do you think of that?"—if you are wondering about a child's immediate reactions.
  - "That's *too* much!" or "That's not true."—if you have strong feelings about something that you consider children should be advised about.
  - "I like that!"—to express your own opinions.

- Another way to share reactions during programs is to have everyone use Message Cards.

HELPFUL THINGS TO DO

Message Cards

Message Cards can serve as temporary communication bridges during a show. Explain that they are used as signals. Custom-fit them to your family's specific needs. Make two kinds of sets: yours and the children's. It might be best to make individual sets for each child.

Your set should consist of warnings, opinions, and explanations, such as:

Can't be done	Ridiculous	Right on
Only half true	Too simple	Well done
Exaggerated	Stereotyped	

Children's set can contain questions or reactions, such as:

Explain	Scary	I like
Make believe?	Why?	Good show
Hard to understand	How?	

For nonreaders, add drawings to the cards.

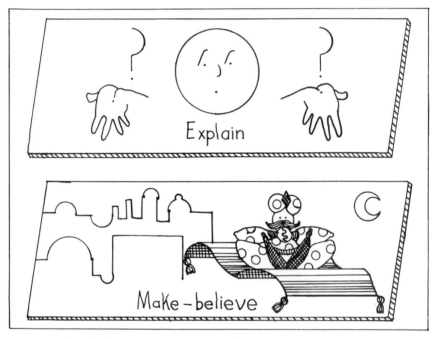

Sample Message Cards

- Try to be casual about your discussions after programs. Avoid bombarding your children with too many questions. Go easy, too, on pushing your own judgments on the children unless you are convinced a program is harmful. Then, in all fairness to them, you must explain what is wrong and why they can no longer turn the program on. Keep in mind that shows about which children are enthusiastic might seem worthless to you. Therein lies the difference between childish and adult taste. If you consider these shows innocuous and do not plan to prohibit your children from watching them, don't spend a lot of time and energy denegrating them. If you do, you run the risk of sounding like a nag; and you might even offend more sensitive children by making a fuss about shows they like, for they can interpret this as a personal put-down.

You will be assuming the role of guide now, always being on the alert to safeguard your family from TV's negative effects and to call their attention to the helpful things they can learn from it. The confusions, misconceptions, and antisocial attitudes with which TV can inundate children are the most difficult for parents to handle. The potentially most confusing and/or harmful aspects of TV programs for children, as cited by researchers, are listed below, together with questions you may wish to consider and use in discussions with your children.

- Aggressive or violent behavior—Was the attacker right to act the way he or she did? Was the behavior too extreme for the situation?
- Antisocial behavior, such as rudeness, humiliation, etc.—What is accomplished by such behavior? Can you think of other ways the people could have acted?
- Stereotyping—The TV description of those people is unfairly exaggerated and limited. In what ways are they like everybody else?
- Depiction of a hero/mentor—What qualities make this character so outstanding? Are the qualities of this character realistic or exaggerated? Is there anything about him or her you would like to copy? Is it sensible, or not, for you to try to copy this character?
- Depiction of a character with whom the child might identify—Is the character someone you would like to have for a friend, or actually be? Why?
- Depiction of a distorted image of the world—In what ways does everyday life for us, and other average people, differ from that shown on TV?
- Sexual behavior—From what you have observed, do you think average people act this way?
- Depiction of a glamorous life-style—Do you imagine that most people have the money, time, and lack of responsibility to lead such carefree lives?
- Oversimplification—Can people solve their problems or accomplish their goals as easily and quickly as shown on TV?
- Depiction of a happy home life—Can family members always be as cooperative as they are on TV?
- Lack of distinction between fantasy and reality—What parts of programs are true to life, and what parts are make-believe?

With practice, and with your persistence, your family will get in the habit of talking about television a great deal. The children will undoubtedly like this. After all, they are crazy about TV, so if it becomes more of a family affair, in a sense they will feel flattered. Your attention to what they deem important will shorten some of the psychological distance between you.

Parents complain often that children prefer "junk" television, refusing to watch more educational or enriching programs such as documentaries or concerts, for example. One way to solve this problem is to introduce Program Swapping, which is designed to broaden the scope of the family's TV viewing. Explain that this activity is for exploration, and not meant to be punishment. A fringe benefit of Program Swapping is that in some instances it might solve family fights over which of several shows to select when there is a time conflict for use of the set. As always in trying new activities, it is advisable to proceed slowly. Gauge the family's tolerance for this new procedure. If your children feel you are overimposing your own taste on them, they will become resistant. Choose lighter, fast-paced types of programs in the beginning.

HELPFUL THINGS TO DO

Program Swapping

At least once a week, each person selects a favorite program the rest of the family must watch. If anyone is on a *TV Turn Off* regime of limited hours, an equal amount of their regular viewing time is sacrificed.

- Rotate turns.
- Decide in advance about specific Program Swaps.
- Talk about family reactions after each show.
- Make Program Swap Charts to be checked and initialed after each show.
- Plan to watch at least two to three different shows of the program before making final decisions about whether to continue watching it or not.

Favorite program choices are often indicative of a person's psychological needs. An example of this could be "The Incredible Hulk" representing power and strength to children who feel relatively helpless and weak. As you watch with your family, think about the following points in reference to each member:

- Why is this program the favorite one?
- Could peer-group pressure possibly have influenced this selection? Does the child really like the show?
- What does the show offer each child: excitement? vicarious "kicks"? escape?
- Does each child understand the story line, if any?
- To what parts of the show does each child react the most?
- Who are each child's favorite characters? Is there any connection between them and the child's personality and/or interests?

PROGRAM SWAP MEET

	Good	So-so	Poor	Bad
Program Chosen By Whom Date				
Program Chosen By Whom Date				
Program Chosen By Whom Date				
Program Chosen By Whom Date				
Program Chosen By Whom Date				

Sample Program Swap Chart

- What do the characters portray—for example, courage a child might like to possess, some type of skill, or what?
- Do the characters seem to be mentors? Does the child identify in some way with them?

Your use of favorite programs as barometers may reveal or reaffirm individual needs about which you can do something immediately and fairly easily. With the main clues you have found, create opportunities for whatever need fulfillment they seem to show. This attempt will of necessity be an experience of trial and error, but it is certainly worth the effort. You cannot compete with the extremes supplied by television, but at least you can help vary the caliber of your children's lives, even if only a little.

Below is a brief rundown of a few of the most common needs that turn people to TV, with suggestions for how to satisfy them.

- A need for a feeling of power—Give the child more responsibilities, geared to his or her capabilities.
- A need for a feeling of competence—Encourage the child to improve skills already acquired and to try new ones.
- A need for escape—Try to vary daily routines based on what the child likes to do best (aside from TV). Try new projects, customs, foods, whatever.
- A need for more interesting pursuits—Introduce new games, ideas for hobbies, small trips in the neighborhood, downtown, to the country, and so forth.
- A need for excitement and adventure—Find appropriate books to be read by or to the child, or for shared reading (both of you read, then discuss). Go on hikes or trips to new places.
- A need for human warmth—Offer more of yours. Encourage visits to and from friends.
- A need for humor—Purposefully look at the funny side of things. Try yourself and encourage the family to take the inconsequential events of life less seriously.

When adults watch television with children, they can perform another very important service: that of helping children learn to sift reality from fantasy. Young children, about seven years and younger, and even some older children who are heavy viewers, have difficulty distinguishing between the two realms. There are several reasons for this. The most obvious are immaturity and lack of experience. There is also the problem of how large a percentage of a child's knowledge of human behavior, events, facts, and places is circumscribed by TV. Those children whose free time is devoted primarily to television accept its world as a real one, often the one they know best. Once involved in a program, a susceptible child envisions it as real; the more the program is seen, the more this impression of realism is reinforced. Television assaults children unremittingly, with tremendous impact, teaching their impressionable minds and leaving strong traces in their memory banks. The result can be a distorted view of life.

The business of unlearning something already learned is hard. Remember this as you help your children analyze the differences between fact and fiction. Often a show portrays such a close combination of the two that even more sophisticated children (and some adults) can be confused or deceived.

There are three steps to take. The following suggestions are broad ones; it is up to you to fill in details according to individual children's levels of comprehension. It might be judicious to start with the assumption that your children are not altogether certain of the fine differences between truth and fiction. Until you get repeated proof that they are aware of them, continue your guidance.

First, use examples from literature, particularly books with which your children are familiar, to talk about fiction. Stress how the art of effective storytelling often includes exaggeration, drama, make-believe, oversimplification, unusualness, exoticism, and similar techniques. Next, discuss your children's favorite TV shows in the same way. Help the children identify specific incidents of fantasy. Describe how these same scenes could be treated in a more realistic fashion.

When the children seem to understand the differences between fact and fantasy, as a second step ask them to spot fantasy on television. Only help when they seem confused or miss examples. You might ask them to embellish on the fantasy by adding their own ideas, together or individually.

HELPFUL THINGS TO DO

Fantasy One-Upmanship

Fantasy One-Upmanship has the dual purpose of giving children more experience with the concept of fantasy and encouraging them to use their own creativity.

Suggest that each child select a fantasy theme and expand on it in any of the following ways:

storytelling	writing a story
playacting	preparing a TV script
pantomiming	drawing
dancing	improvising music or rhythms

The third step is the hardest, as it necessitates separating exaggerated and unlikely events from a seemingly true-to-life background. Many situation comedies use a mixture of reality and fiction. This also occurs in fictional- ized documentaries, called docudramas, which are even more difficult to analyze. Start by explaining that the tradition of American TV production is to entertain and/or attract audiences by any means. This entails many questionable practices, justified under the umbrella of dramatic license, such as making overstatements or understatements; leaving out important facts; telling half-truths; stereotyping; and so on. Point out whatever discrepancies you find on TV between fact and falsehood. Talk about them with your family. Tell the children that the portrayal of human behavior on TV worries you because so much of it is inaccurate. Select a familiar show. Before watching together, suggest the children plan to look for:

- how people treat each other
- how people scheme and plot
- how people solve problems
- exaggerated or unusual behavior
- the impossibility/improbability of some events

After the program, discuss all of the points. In addition, ask the children to consider these additional ones:

- Did you notice anything that made you uneasy?
- What would you have done had you been in that situation?
- Do you have any suggestions for other ways to handle the dilemmas that occurred?
- How do you feel about the way people treated each other?
- Do you believe that some or all of the behavior shown is true to life?

Parallel television viewing by parents and children is *the* thing to do, of- fering so many benefits to the development of children's understanding of human behavior both on the screen and in reality. The practice started in this chapter of talking together about programs is carried to a deeper level in the next, where activities are outlined for analyzing all aspects of TV fare as well as family problems.

TV-Springboard for Family Discussions

○ ○ ○

6

If you have already done some of the Helpful Things to Do, you have had practice in using television for family talks. In this chapter we shall be stressing this custom. Because of the very controversial and varied subjects that are part of usual TV fare, the medium lends itself to constant postmortems. Even though some of the things we are subjected to by TV are disturbing, and even more so for children than for adults, notwithstanding we can be grateful to TV for bringing some of them to our attention. Because children are first introduced through TV to many concepts that are ordinarily associated with adult living, we are forced into talking about them. In the long run this may well serve to our advantage. You may find yourself in conversations with your children about subjects that were taboo between parent and child when you were growing up. Perhaps you were confused or upset about something but did not dare approach your parents for clarification or reassurance. Television has been partially responsible (the rest of the mass media are also responsible) for breaking down the barrier that once existed between the generations. Children have always managed to find out about a great many adult activities despite parental efforts to prolong their children's innocence. Now we are more realistic about children's precocity, knowing full well they are being exposed to raw life via the TV set! We might as well take advantage of the springboard it gives us for frank discussions.

We agree that it can be rough to air feelings about sex, violence, or other emotionally loaded behavior that appears in a program. Many parents are

49

reluctant to enter into dialogues with their children about these topics. If this is your initial reaction, try to overcome it. Assume that your children may be harmed by what they see and that you *can* prevent this from happening by involving them in talks. The more you share your ideas and knowledge about touchy issues, the better prepared your children will be for coping with life. If you look at it this way, you will be able to take the first plunge; after that, it does get easier.

HELPFUL THINGS TO DO

Difficult Dialogue Practice

As suggested in Rehearsal Role Playing in Chapter 2, it does help to playact anticipated difficult encounters in advance. There are several ways you can do this:

• Talk about it with your spouse or another interested adult.
• If you are at a loss for how to explain something, find a book for parents that can give you guidelines.
• Plan what you will say and how you will put it into words.
• Practice an imaginary conversation with your family. Do this as many times as it takes for you to feel more comfortable about the prospect of an actual confrontation of this kind.

Although most of the things you will be discussing will be of a serious nature, do all that you can to prevent these family sessions from becoming too oppressive. Mention at the start that your goal is to pool information and ideas. Explain also that you want to rid the children of whatever confusions or misconceptions they may have. You might even tell them that you wish your own parents had included these kinds of subjects in the talks they held with you when you were a child.

Before you start, go over the following rules of thumb for the art of clear person-to-person communication. If you aren't already following these, incorporate them into your discussions. Encourage the rest of the family to use them, for they really do facilitate understanding one another.

Listening
• If you don't understand what the other person means, ask "Can you tell me that in different words? I don't quite know what you mean," or "This is what I heard you say [give specifics]. Is that what you meant?"
• Watch the other person's nonverbal behavior (such as eye and facial expressions, hand movements, etc.) and note voice tones, pitch, rate of speech, etc. to "read" the full impact of his or her message.
• Allow each person adequate time for self-expresssion.

Speaking
- Use as simple, brief, and clear messages as you can.
- If using new words, define them. Be certain children know what you are talking about.
- Ask listeners to repeat back to you what you said to be sure they understood your message.

Keeping Channels of Communication Open
- Be open-minded. Respect each person's opinions.
- Encourage family members to state their own opinions and feelings before telling them yours.
- Avoid making long speeches. Try to maintain an even give-and-take between everyone.
- Try to ascertain everyone's moods before starting these conversations. Strong reluctance on their part may defeat your purpose. Bide your time until you think all are willing to participate.

There are a variety of ways to implement significant talks sparked by TV, in addition to regularly planned discussions. It is good to schedule the latter, however, so that you keep in close touch with what your children are absorbing from the programs they see.

HELPFUL THINGS TO DO

Spontaneous Spotting

While watching TV, keep a pad and pencil handy so that you can jot down incidents you want to discuss. Encourage the children to do this also, telling them to list anything about which they are confused or that they suspect you would like to talk over. Try to cover the list as soon as possible while details are still fresh in everyone's minds.

Important Issues

There may be topics you have never or seldom talked about with your family that you feel should be aired in discussion, especially if they concern matters included in the programs your children are watching.

- Start with what worries you the most.
- Ask the children to tell you all that they know about the subject, and what their feelings and attitudes are.
- Correct any misinformation that they may have gathered.

- State your thoughts and opinions.
- Ask frequently for feedback from your children.
- Encourage them to keep talking with you until you feel their understanding has improved and you have treated the subject in as much depth as is appropriate.
- Bring up the same topic from time to time to be sure the children are not confused or upset by it.

Real Life Isn't That Way

The fantasy of television *cannot be overemphasized.* The more opportunities your family has to extract the make-believe elements out of programs, the more discerning viewers they will be.

- Start out with programs that seem almost believable but that you feel give a false impression to children.
- Analyze each show as thoroughly as you can. Take advantage of commercial breaks to talk about discrepancies. Help your childen spot the fine areas between reality and fantasy.

In Real Life

In Real Life can follow Real Life Isn't That Way. It contrasts fact with fantasy and can be helpful with younger children.

- Retell a program's plot with a true-to-life version.
- Ask children to compare your version with the show's version and find the difference.
- Ask children to make up their own versions of a more realistic plot.

Become A Favorite Character

For some children, favorite characters are more than just that. They become idols and mentors. This activity will give you insight as to how important a character is to your child and at the same time will help the child gain a little more objectivity about the character.

- Ask the child to select a favorite character to imitate.
- Assume the role of another character in the same show to interact with and enrich your child's role playing.

- Help your child assemble any costume parts or props that will make playacting more enjoyable.
- Playact as much as possible. Ask other family members to play other characters, or use pillows, dolls, stuffed or real animals, brooms, and so on to represent them.
- Talk over characters' behavior and actions. Compare these with the child's usual behavior. If there are any controversial aspects to the character's relationship with others, talk about these and in your playacting try to provoke incidents for your child's reactions through role playing.
- Do this same kind of thing, suggesting that your child role play disliked characters.
- For variation, tell your child to role play characters and then have the family guess who they are.

Host A Favorite Character

Your family will probably enjoy this and at the same time reveal to you just how they interpret everyday life.

- Ask the family to decide on a character from a TV show, such as Mork of *Mork and Mindy,* or to make up a similar imaginary person who comes from a different place to visit with you.
- To represent that character, use something fairly large such as a big cushion, bolster, broom, or box, or make a Supercolossal Rag Doll. (See directions at end of this activity).
- Include the character in all family activities: set a place at the table for it; take it on rides; give it bed space; find it a spot in front of the TV set.
- Ask the children to explain and interpret everything that is going on to the character, pretending everything is new to it. Especially encourage them to explain the TV shows they watch.

Directions for Making a Supercolossal Rag Doll
- Use an old sheet (which can be dyed for skin color) or any large material remnant.
- Make the head by stuffing the top part with paper, material scraps, or foam-rubber bits. Try to fashion a lifesize or slightly bigger-than-life head. After it is stuffed, wrap the base with string or large elastic bands.
- Add features by using felt markers, or embroidering or sewing them on.
- Attach old dust mops, feather dusters, or thick strands of yarn for hair. Be sure to fasten these firmly.

- Dress the doll in real clothes: smock; shirt; nightgown; sweater; etc. Attach firmly.
- If you prefer a doll with backbone, insert a thick dowel stick or moderate-sized broom handle before wrapping the neck.
- You can make smaller versions by stuffing old panty hose, tying the top end, then wrapping the neck, and so on.

Super Colossal   Panty-Hose

Sample Rag Dolls

Find Yourself In TV

TV programs often portray incidents and reactions similar to those we experience. Use these to start family talks to gain a better understanding of one another.

Mood Analysis.   Look for reasons why you suppose characters have different moods and compare them to your own by saying, for instance, "That mother sighs a lot about her children. Sometimes I feel that way, too, because . . . " Encourage the rest of the family to do the same thing.

Vicarious "kicks" or Borrowed Daydreaming. Ask provocative que\. tions, such as "That boy rides his bike all over town; do you wish you could, too?"

Identification. Point out any aspects of television characters' personalities that remind you of yourself. Ask the family if they can spot them, then talk about them. Try this with everybody.

Role Preparation. TV gives us a constant stream of models, both worthwhile and undesirable, that cover just about every kind of role imaginable, from family life, ages and stages of development, occupations, and so forth. These models appear in shows and commercials and are usually clearly defined and easy to identify. Talk about these, and suggest to the children that they playact some of the mannerisms of the different roles.

TV As Textbook

Television is encyclopedic in that it covers such a wide range of subjects relevant to everyday lives. Tap this source to discuss situations as objectively as possible. You can custom-fit these topics to the immediate needs of your family, use them as they appear on the screen, or search for examples that will lead to specific themes you have in mind. Listed below are samples of some of the most common subjects that are helpful for family discussions:

Parent-Child Relationships—parental expectations; aspirations; styles; communication skills; obligations; mutual respect; compatability; affection; mutual enjoyment.

Sibling Relationships—competition; fighting; jealousy; friendship; mutual acceptance; admiration; antagonism; protectiveness.

Extended Family Relationships—family loyalty; mutual help; sustained interest; mutual respect.

Family Discipline—autocratic; democratic; laissez-faire; punishment; respect; fear; caring; overprotection.

Family Boundaries—individual independence; accountability; friends; outside activities.

Sex Roles in the Family—specific expectations; designated areas; responsibilities; rigidity; flexibility.

Privacy in the Family—Nonexistent; respected.

Meaning of Family—closeness; separateness; nurturance; constriction; strong ties; tenuous affiliation.

Cooperation in the Family—assumed; forced; bargained for; spasmodic; in crises.

Responsibility in the Family—responsibility for self; commitment to family members; sacrifice; generosity.

Family Problems—shared; children spared; overwhelming; coped with.

Difficult Family Members—handled with care; tolerated; ignored; scapegoated; catered to.

Materialism—overemphasized; controlled; take it or leave it.

Cars—how used; for what purposes.

Firearms—why; when to use; how to use.

Drugs—when needed; peer pressure; dangers.

Fads—transiency; cost.

Prejudice—self-defeating; how acquired; how overcome.

World of Work—careers; success; compromise.

Education—why needed; perseverance; rewards.

Family Mix-Match

You can use something from TV to start this, or do it at any time. The purpose is to help each person get a mirrored self-portrait reflected by other family members, playacted impressions. Discuss ahead of time the possibility that some of these may be nonflattering. Suggest that good sportsmanship be the name of the game.

- Switch seats at the supper table, such as mother sitting in daughter's seat, daughter in son's, and so on.
- Each person playacts the replaced person's behavior.
- Talk about what happened afterwards.
- Repeat Mix-Match frequently.

Air Clearers

Air Clearers is an extended version of Family Mix-Match. Its purpose is to provide safety valves when family members are upset with one another. This is accomplished by using a variety of props to act as buffers in the resolution of family feuds. These same things might prove effective if used with shy people who find it difficult to enter into group or one-to-one conversations.

- Set aside a special place for storage of Air Clearers.
- Air Clearers can be puppets, Supercolossal Rag Dolls, dolls or stuffed animals, cushions, beanbags, paper dolls (the larger, the better), or Mammoth Masks (described below).
- Whenever a fight is brewing, encourage everyone to use an Air Clearer as a "front" to talk over or playact a way to avoid or resolve the problem.
- Air Clearers also can be adapted to rehearse appropriate behavior for anticipated difficult situations such as self-defense, asserting one's rights, getting along with people in nasty moods, etc.

Directions for Mammoth Masks

• Masks can be made to resemble family members (including pets), other people, animals, imaginary creatures.
• Make the Masks either life-size or larger-than-life.
• There are three types: fitted over the head; covering the face; covering only the eyes.
• Different facial expressions can be used; for example, you could make a set of eyes happy; mad; glaring; sleepy; amazed; etc. On the bags you can make a two-sided Mask, one side smiling, the other frowning.
• Materials: heavy paper; large grocery bags; cardboard; construction paper covered with clear contact paper; fabric pasted on cardboard; and so on. Use crayons or felt pens to decorate, or paste or sew on features. Use wool or lengths of shredded fabric for hair.
• Handles: these can be made of double layers of cardboard; thin dowel sticks; chopsticks; unsharpened pencils; rolled corrugated cardboard; etc.

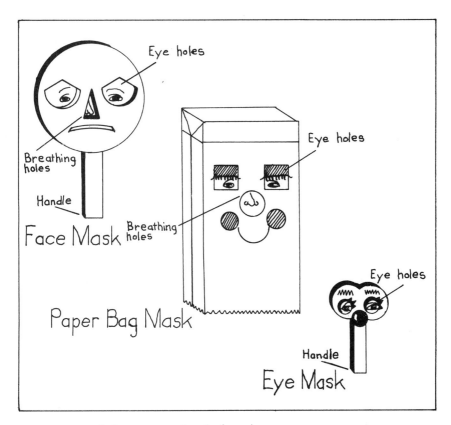

Sample Mammoth Masks

Tricky TV

The purpose of Tricky TV is to add new dimensions to the experience of television and provide the family the chance to do some playacting in accompaniment to TV.

No Sound—Turn off the sound and have everyone improvise dialogue and sound effects while watching the visuals.

No Picture—Turn off the visuals but leave on the sound. Everyone interprets the action from listening to the sound.

Turn Off TV—Turn On Books

Use every possible occasion after TV-generated family discussions to find relevant books. They can give depth to whatever subject you may cover. Use the books (or any other appropriate reading material) in several ways:

- Ask the children to read them and to talk about what they read.
- Read to the children, and then discuss.
- If the children are unable to or won't read, read the material yourself and report back to the family.

The establishment of easy-flowing family dialogues opens new avenues of mutual understanding between parents and children. With television as a point of departure, such talks become valuable learning and sharing experiences for everyone.

Because television is so emotionally provocative, you are well advised to stay in close touch with children's reactions to what they view. The following chapter offers ways to handle TV hangovers.

TV - The Emotional Mix Master

o o o

Television really is an emotional mix-master. It churns our feelings around and around, then stops abruptly in midstream for a commercial. Often our emotions are spinning at such a rate that it takes several seconds to accommodate to the vast difference between the dramatic effects of a show and the sponsor's mundane message. For impressionable people, children in particular, the constant emotional bombardment of TV can be undermining.

There are several reasons why television exerts such power over our emotional reactions. The most obvious of these is the craftsmanship used for dramatic effect and the creation of illusions. Like the cinema, TV can affect us through a myriad of devices. However, TV is unique in that we use it in the privacy of our homes. Seated in our comfortable chairs, surrounded by all the accoutrements of our daily existence that enable us to relax and lower our inhibitions, we are easy targets for television's emotionality.

No one knows for certain what TV viewing might be doing to our emotional stability. As emotional "sitting ducks," are we being somewhat incapacitated by it? Does it somehow erode our emotional mechanism, interfering with our ability to react normally in real life? Does it plant an undue amount of anxiety or malaise in us? Is TV really an electronic Svengali, often reducing us to a kind of emotional blank with its weird, unbalanced form of emotional stimulation? Whatever is going on, it is important to become more perceptive of your family's emotional reactions to television.

59

In order to gauge television's impact on us emotionally, it is necessary to consider its effect on our total beings. Our physical, social, and intellectual status will also influence our emotional condition, and vice versa. We bring the components of our individual well-being or lack of well-being to the set each time we settle down in front of it. Our physical condition can affect our reaction to TV viewing: Are we too full of food, or hungry? How about our fatigue level—are we tired, fidgety, in need of activity? It is a good idea to know our social "temperature" at the time we watch TV, too. Various aspects of how we believe we are getting along with others can color our approach to TV. The caliber of our ongoing relationships with family members takes precedence here. This will be intertwined with our self-images and the amount of self-confidence and satisfaction with our lives we feel at the moment. Also of significance are the residues of feelings simmering in us as a result of our most recent encounters with other people: did things go well or not? The compatibility of our intellectual needs and TV fare must be considered too. This is difficult to determine, as people are not generally aware of being intellectually deprived or inadequately stimulated. It boils down to this: if we don't have much of interest to think about and are bogged down in repetitious or petty thoughts, we need a provocative, challenging spark. What if television keeps disappointing us?

The kind of mood we bring to television is a potpourri of conditions within us, most of which we do not always realize. This is what we might be feeling, vaguely or acutely, *before* our exposure. During and after watching, our entire outlooks, and even our awareness of some hitherto hidden sensations and attitudes, might change, for better or for worse. What is rather upsetting in terms of all of this is that TV may not actually satisfy us. It captures our attention but often leaves us somewhat empty. This is the risk we run by watching. Is the possible invasion on our emotions too big a price to pay for what television gives us?

AWARENESS ACTIVITY

Take Your Emotional Pulse

This exercise will help you understand the manipulative effect of TV. As you study its effect on yourself, you will gain more empathy for what it does to your children.

- *Before* you watch, think about:
  Your mood;
  Your preoccupations;
  Your anxieties;
  Your physical state.

- *After* you watch, consider:
  Your mood;
  What is uppermost in your thoughts;
  Your physical state;
  Your preference for what to do next.

It is important to mention that not all of the emotional upheavals television inflicts upon us are harmful, however. It can also serve as a beneficial catharsis. Like any other form of mass media, it offers us an outlet for pent-up feelings, often helping us heal ourselves by causing us to laugh uproariously; cry unreservedly; identify momentarily with someone we feel is a "kindred soul"; become exhilarated and uplifted; achieve vicarious vendettas by hearing others attack our favorite "hates"; gain a breather from reality through escape. TV offers many variations of emotional experiences that touch each of us idiosyncratically.

Let's look a little more thoroughly now at some of the ways television can work on our emotions. The method by which it is delivered to us can often disarm us. It thrusts tightly packaged, concentrated segments of action at us, frequently a mixture of dubious fact and fiction, that simultaneously assault our eyes, ears, minds, and hearts. Sometimes what we see is not something we would have chosen to witness or necessarily would have been exposed to in the ordinary course of our lives. Even though this is truer for children than for adults, nonetheless we all can be unprepared for some of the things that have become a common part of the TV genre. Since much of this comes to us with an unrelenting rapidity, it can leave many viewers defenseless, unable to cope momentarily with the combined intellectual and emotional sensationalism. Confusion results, with the rationale for things left hanging and unresolved.

It is such a one-sided affair; there we are, being fed all this difficult-to-fathom content, unable to do much with it but allow it to pelt our senses and common sense and often to fill us with disullusion and despair. This can be emotionally draining.

The caliber of many TV programs is the same, despite the variety in the formats and episodes presented. The concepts that are included remain relatively static; hence there is a great deal of repetition to the emotions that are aroused by our watching. After a while, this has a tendency to blur our sensibilities and deaden our reactions. It is a matter of getting used to the same old story; after a time, numbness can set in. We adults have had enough experience to maintain some immunity to this insidious danger. Our children, however, can be harmed. Whether we like it or not, TV can be a more effective teacher than all of the interested adults in a child's environment. Because children accept TV as such an important source of information, their knowledge of the world can become greatly distorted through it. Much of what they see and accept so unequivocally can interfere with their developing sense of humanity. The fact that this can be happening unbe-knownst to us, their caring parents, is a threat we dare not overlook.

AWARENESS ACTIVITY

Put The TV Experience In Perspective

This quick Awareness Activity is for the whole family, not only the adults. Its purpose is to make everyone more conscious of how TV works on our emotions.

Compare viewing a dramatic TV program with reading (or being read to, for nonreaders) a book of a similar kind, in relation to:

- Feelings aroused during and afterwards.
- How much time and opportunity we have for thinking and analyzing the plot while exposed to it.
- Differences between written and television characterizations, settings, and other details.
- How much of a story is easily recalled.
- Overall reactions to both media as entertainment.

We know that some television can take us away from ourselves in a way, catapulting us into a kind of limbo. It is as if we are as bound in and im-mobilized as the pills in a bottle, the top of which is stuffed tight with cot-ton. Even when the bottle is shaken, the pills cannot move. Scientists call this an ''alpha state.'' Our most immediate concern with this is how to snap out of it. How each person emerges is a very individualized matter. The re-entry to ongoing existence is harder for some than for others. The process requires a readjustment, even if infinitesimal, to the surrounding social en-vironment; it can be compared to the culture shock people feel when return-ing home after a prolonged stay in another country! They have to take hold of themselves to regain normal habit patterns in interaction with others and to do what is expected of them. This effort, combined with the emotions sparked by what has been viewed on TV, can make the return to reality a difficult, slow journey. To put it rather bluntly, it necessitates a metamor-phosis from TV zombie back to human being. Many people, in an am-biguous condition as they emerge, feel quite uncomfortable. This can be spotted by their irritability, taciturnity, combustibility, or restlessness.

HELPFUL THINGS TO DO
Half-Way Space

Here are ideas to help ease TV hangovers.

• Allow everyone several minutes of uncluttered time for "cooling off" after leaving the set. Don't hassle them; try to prevent them from hassling you by not reacting to their moods.
• Designate a special, fairly private spot where a person can go until feeling sociable once again. Call this the Half-Way Space, explaining that it is a neutral place where a person's desire to be left alone will be honored.
• When individuals rejoin the family, welcome them and talk with them about what they have been viewing, feeling, thinking, etc.

Another indirect way in which television affects emotional well-being is the time and attention it steals from normal family conversations and togetherness. Family communication and closeness are jeopardized by lessened opportunities for interaction. TV, the family's favorite possession, surreptitiously separates family members from one another. The best antidote for this is to talk as much as possible with each other, at all times, about everything, television and its effects most especially.

HELPFUL THINGS TO DO
Hot-Topics Tourney

Hot Topics Tourney is a quick verbal airing activity, meant to serve as a family safety-valve for TV-generated emotions.

• Select TV characters, names, TV incidents and/or scenes, or TV-related family rules or concerns, such as "The Incredible Hulk"; shooting; no TV after 8 *P.M.*
• Take one topic at a time and cover it in depth.
• Allow each person to talk about it without interruption.
• Encourage everyone to express feelings.
• Try to alleviate any confusions or anxieties by explanations and reassurances.

Why is television so irresistible to so many? If you look at some of the underlying reasons for TV's enduring hold on people, you may gain an insight here and there that will help you understand your own family's fondness for it. This information may make it easier for you to partially separate or unhook from its powerful magnetism those most addicted to it.

For most people who have grown up with TV, it is an integral part of their life experiences. The set has always been there. Their use of it is a habit formed since early childhood, perhaps even during infancy. It has taken such prominence in their daily lives (and even in the scheme of things for those who grew up before the late 1940s when it was introduced in this country) that it is placed high on their list of customary activities. People who have always known TV have learned to depend on it for a variety of reasons: it is recreation; it is a way to pass time; it offers a form of companionship; it is an escape, and it is just about the most effortless thing one can do; it is even more instantaneous than falling asleep!

Television has turned out to be one of the most effective of all instantaneous panaceas discovered by man. Each one of us turns to TV for our own special reasons, sometimes without ever being completely conscious of *why* we need to. Some of the main motivations are to:

- use TV as a way to become disinvolved with the present
- get a vacation from exerting oneself in any way
- put a wedge between people so we don't have to face one another
- obtain instant amusement
- put some excitement in otherwise rather dull lives
- seek out our mentors and idols (this is especially important to children)
- be on the receiving end of a process that makes no demands of us whatsoever

Television is dependably always available; it is a very tempting sorcerer that few can resist. It often offers the path of least resistance.

The following activities are intended to offer more opportunities for your family to work through some of the emotional turmoil that may be brought on by television.

HELPFUL THINGS TO DO

Self-Stocktaking

Self-Stocktaking is a combined appraisal of TV's effect, immediately after leaving the set and over a long term.

Ask yourselves these questions right after TV:

- How do I feel?
- What would I like most to do now?

- Can I trace any connections between how I feel and what I just saw?
- As a result, do I feel any of the following:

anxious	dissatisfied	depressed	delighted	fascinated
fearful	frustrated	angry	optimistic	challenged
guilty	bored	tired	happy	inspired
confused	envious	restless	smarter	nervous

Suggest that everyone make a personal TV and Feelings Chart, using the above feelings or any others they prefer. Plan to fill in these charts over a period of several weeks or longer. Use the charts to talk over and decide whether it might be kinder to your emotional systems to eliminate certain programs.

CODE: SUE'S TV AND FEELINGS CHART
Happy □ Confused ◙ Uneasy ⊟ Sad   ▣ Inspired ◪ Tired   ◩
Fearful ◪ Nervous ⊡ Smarter ⊞ Bored ■ Angry ▣ Depressed ▤

Mon.	Tues.	Wed.	Thurs.	Fri.	Sat.	Sun.
Week of 4/9 I Love Lucy □ Rookies⊟ Little House □	Brady B.□ Adam 12 ◙ Happy Days. □	Brady B. ■ Sha Na Na ■ Jeffersons □	Gunsmoke ⊟ Ironsides ◪ Muppets □	Bewitched □ Brady B. □ Sanford □ Burnett ■	Marlo □ Bugs □ Outdoors ■ Family Feud Chips ◩	Thats Cat □ Villa □ Magoo □ Wild King Disney ◪
Week of 4/16 My Favorite Martin □ Muppets □ Odd Couple □	Adam 12 ◙ Sanford □ Mash □	Bewitched □ Brady B. □ Eight is Enough ▣	Brady B. □ Mork □ Hawaii 5-0	Gunsmoke ⊟ Adam 12 ◪ Rockford ◩ Files ◪	Chips ◩ Bonanza □ Love Boat ◙	Thats Cat ■ Popeye ■ World of Disney ⊟
Week of						

Sample TV And Feeling Chart

TV Makes Us . . .

TV Makes Us . . . is an extension of Self-Stocktaking. After children leave the TV set, encourage them to express their immediate feelings by:

- acting out, individually or together, their moods
- drawing, painting, or crayoning mood pictures (see Chapter 11)

- clay modeling, using commercial clay or play dough (see Chapter 11)
- writing descriptions, stories, or poems (see Chapter 10)
- creating mood music or rhythms by using their voices; their hands; a real instrument; a homemade instrument such as an instant drum (beating on anything with hand, spoon, etc.) (see Chapter 11)

TV Blues Cure

Make small prescription cards for children to carry as reminders, or leave these posted in a prominent spot near the TV set. Occasionally check with the children to be sure they are following their recommended cures.

TV BLUES CURE

PRESCRIPTION   DATE: April 10, 1981.

FOR: Sue

REASON:

    To cure nervousness.
    To get rid of bad dreams.
    To put in a happier mood.

WHAT TO DO:

    Do not watch scary programs.
    Do not ask friends about scary programs missed.

DOSAGE:

    Repeat daily until feeling better.

SIGNED: Concerned Mother

Sample Prescription

First Aid For Fears

The purpose of this activity is exactly what its name suggests: to give emotional first aid for TV-generated fears.

• Encourage everyone to mention anything from television that has been upsetting.
• Each person's fear is acted out by the others. The fear's "owner" is free to discuss the playacting, request changes, or enter into it.
• After the person is satisfied that all parts of the fear as experienced have been covered, there should be a discussion of what occurred.

The combination of stating the fear, seeing it acted out, and talking about it often helps reduce the fear. This same technique can be used with any type of emotion that TV arouses.

Back To The Real World

This kind of activity is useful as an antidote to TV's spell. There are two versions to it; suggest them to your family:

Outdoors:—Right after TV, go outside. Plan to do something active such as jogging, playing with a friend, riding a bike, building a house of twigs or pebbles, throwing a ball.

Indoors—After TV, do exercises, jog in place, turn on some music and dance to it, find something useful to do such as pare vegetables for supper, vacuum, dust the house (TV set included), talk with the family, or read.

Mini-TV

A Mini-TV is a miniature, homemade reproduction of a TV screen and whatever characters, props, or scenes with which a child is familiar. It can be adapted to individual or family needs.

The purpose of this is to give the children a set of easy-to-handle materials with which they can play out some of their reactions to TV programs. It is especially recommended for preschool children but can be useful for people of all ages.

Directions For Making a Mini-TV

A screen or flannel board can be purchased in a teacher's supply or toy store, or you can make your own by covering heavy cardboard at least 18″ by 18″ (the bigger the better) with flannel, turkish toweling, velvet, or a sheet of thin foam rubber. You can also use a magnet board.

Characters and props can be cut out of flannel, pelon, toweling, any heavy material, or paper. To make them stick to the board, experiment by putting on the backs strips of two-sided Scotch tape, thin sandpaper, or large paper clips if using a magnet board. If freehand drawing is hard for you, cut the pictures out of magazines, newspapers, or coloring books, or trace pictures from books. If these are flimsy, mount them on thin cardboard, perhaps covering them with clear contact paper to make them more durable; then attach whatever adhesive material works to the back, as suggested above.

The custom of recognizing and immediately dealing with moods generated by television is an effective way to maintain family peace. It also puts in perspective the kind and degree of influence that viewing exerts on individuals.

Children need to know what a big business the television industry is and some of the complexities of production. That's what the next chapter is about.

Put TV Under
the Microscope

8

o o o

The plan to take a closer look at television can turn out to be fascinating research for the family. There are several ways to do this, all of them offering opportunities for everyone's participation, no matter what their ages. You can form a home research team to do a long-term study on how the Magic Lantern casts its spell. Your main laboratory will be centered around your set(s) from which you will get most of the material you will want to analyze. To round out your study, you may want to watch for magazine and newspaper articles or books that discuss the business aspects of the TV industry.

When you put TV under a microscope, you and your family gain in three major ways. The first of these is that such a study is a challenging, mind-opening process that is basically educational but can be fun as well. The second payoff is less obvious but equally important. That concerns your role as teacher to your children. Your guidance to enable them to become more knowledgeable about TV's tricks is an invaluable service to them. It should also help alleviate some of the guilt you may have about allowing TV to become so important to them. The third gain is a combination of the other two. The more your family discovers about the inner workings of the TV you watch, the less influence it will have on you. A little bit of disillusionment, particularly among your chldren, can go a long way. It may turn all of you into a more discriminating audience!

To convince you of how worthwhile this type of TV nitpicking can be, I have listed some of the specific benefits that can accrue to your children:

- The more your children understand how TV works, the more easily they will be able to differentiate between fact and fantasy.
- An in-depth scrutiny of TV can help your children put it in proper perspective in relation to their other life experiences. They may learn to value TV less in contrast to more self-generated activities.
- The more aware your children are of how TV glosses over, exaggerates, understates, and distorts the truth in other ways, the less gullible they will be in accepting TV fare as a reliable source of information.
- The more discerning and critical viewers your children are, the less easily they will be exploited, particularly by commercials.
- The clearer your children's comprehension about TV's powerful sensationalism, the less apt they are to be upset by some of what they view.

A possible fringe benefit to parents may be that with this more concentrated appraisal of the medium, you may continually find *yourselves* aroused enough to be undaunted in your crusade to protect your family from TV's nefarious side effects.

It may be difficult at the start, even for adults, to be disassociated enough from watching and listening to critique what is happening. Most television is more of an emotional than an intellectual experience; therefore the average viewer has not learned to think much about the process while exposed to it. Usually reflection takes place afterwards and concerns a reaction that is more general than specific. It may be wise for you to practice dissecting several shows by yourself to get the feel for it before you mention the idea to the family.

Be prepared, too, that even though your children may well be intrigued by the research plan and may want to cooperate, it may turn out to be a struggle for certain individuals. A lot will depend on how deeply involved a person becomes when watching TV. Some people are totally carried away and cannot be distracted. If that is the case at your house, then an alternate approach is to talk about your research "findings" right after the program so that the child will understand them second hand. The awareness of what is under discussion will influence the child's viewing reactions. In time, this information might even nibble away at the child's total absorption in front of the set. You can anticipate that it can act as a wedge to somewhat free the child from the hold TV has on his or her attention.

Let us remind ourselves once again of the forceful pull television exerts on most of us. It impells us to concentrate on it by almost totally involving our senses of sight and hearing. Once our attention is caught, we are bombarded with such a continuity of rapid sound and movement that we get carried along, sometimes almost witlessly. There we are, caught in the mesmerizing arms of this sirenlike electronic device, wallowing in a kind of trance. We are not called upon to do anything more than turn on a switch to cause this constant stream of entertainment to pass before us. We give ourselves to it, willingly and repeatedly. It can become irresistable at times for many of us, an amazingly convenient combination of escape, recreation, and time filler. We have to face the fact that for many people TV holds more control of them than they of it. Children are its most vulnerable victims. Learning to be more objective about television will make everyone in your family less vulnerable to TV's allure.

As a preamble to your research, a brief glance at the television industry is in order. The main point never to lose sight of is that TV is *big business.* Money making is its prime objective; everything else is secondary. It goes about making money in a variety of ways, all of which sum up to selling something to the consumers, the trade name for all of us who so accommodatingly buy and use TV sets and watch commercials. And it is not only the actual things advertised on the screen that we buy; it is also a large number of TV-related objects ranging from puppets of TV characters to books based on the most popular TV shows. Television has saturated our culture with an acquisitive itch that knows no bounds. Of course other advertising forms have a part in this, but TV's impact is perhaps the most pervasive.

Everything about television production is expensive. Broadcasting budgets are computed in time segments with the cost being carried through the purchase of minutes, or parts of minutes, by advertisers. These advertisers, or sponsors, may pay hundreds of thousands of dollars for a one-minute spot commercial in what is labeled "prime time," usually evening hours when the audience is the largest. Because these costs are so high and because audience reaction is fairly unpredictable, the whole affair boils down to a form of gambling. With such astronomical stakes, the main production thrust has to aim at catching and holding viewers' attention, no holds barred. As a result of this, a good deal of television programming is conceived and carried out with more of a salesmanship mentality than artistry. The important criterion of a propsed program is its salability to a sponsor, who in turn will judge it from the same vantage point in terms of the viewers rather than value the program as a worthwhile contribution. The national tote board for all this is the A.C. Nielsen Company, a rating service that issues quick reports on the popularity of programs. These ratings carry tremendous weight, despite the fact that they are based on only a small percentage of the viewing audience.

We viewers take for granted what comes on our home TV screens without giving much thought to the tremendous amount of work its production entails. Although credits for specific participation are included either at the start or the end of each program, rarely do we pay much attention to them. Even the longest lists of credit acknowledgment cannot include all the people who have shared in the responsibility of getting a show on the airways. The amount of man and woman power employed and the wide range of talents used are extraordinary when compared to other industries. One marvels at how slick and finished are the shows we see when one realizes the complexity of television production and broadcasting. An endless stream of technically flawless shows flows across our screen despite the pitfalls of the time deadlines, the possibility of human error and lack of cooperation, and the innumerable processes through which each program must progress before completion. By comparison, the steps necessary for the design and manufacture of a superjet plane seem relatively simple!

HELPFUL THINGS TO DO

Looking Behind The Scenes

The introduction of the wide variety of people who work behind the scenes of TV production provides your children with useful background information. It may clarify the cost aspects of each program and may make it easier for them to understand the economic need for the commercials. Perhaps they will be less easily taken in by ads when they realize what a competitive, highly speculative game television really is. Even if such concepts are premature for them, at least they will be interested in the many different skills TV production requires.

The following list includes the most obvious job categories associated with production and broadcasting. Before describing each person's job to your children, ask them what they think it might involve. Then discuss it in more detail with them, emphasizing how closely everyone must cooperate in order to complete a project successfully.

The producer starts the program rolling and is responsible for bringing together the various people who are going to participate.

The writer has to take the producer's idea for the show and write a script. There are many requirements the writer must follow, such as writing short segments to fit in between commercials; including very exciting action just before time for the commercial break in order to be sure the viewer will continue to watch after the break; creating a plot that will reveal a lot of action in a short time period; and so forth.

The director is responsible for helping the producer select the people for the program and for coordinating all aspects of it when it is shot.

The director's most important role is that of turning the script into effective live action.

The casting director has to find the most suitable people who will be selected to act in the show.

Actors and actresses follow the play's script and pretend to be the characters in the story. Some children do not realize that their favorite characters are *at work* on a TV program, and not being televised in their normal lives. Actors and actresses usually hire *Agents* who recommend them for acting jobs.

The set designer has to design and oversee the building of sets. The set designer must also choose the furnishings and other objects that complete the set requirements.

The properties coordinator moves the various parts of the set to accommodate each scene.

The costume designer draws detailed pictures of each costume that will be used.

The costume coordinator has to keep all costumes in order, in good repair, and available for the actors' use.

The makeup artist is responsible for everyone's makeup.

The hairdresser has to arrange all the actors' hair before they go on stage and be responsible for the maintenance of any wigs used.

The music and/or song writer creates and either plays or directs all the music for the show, including theme songs and background music.

Musicians are either solo or orchestras.

The audio engineer arranges for whatever action or background sound effects are required.

The audio mixer controls the volume and tonal quality of whatever sound effects are being picked up on the audio equipment during shooting.

The cameraman has to coordinate the shooting of the visuals under the director's direction.

The lighting designer has to arrange for all lighting effects.

The special effects specialist has to coordinate all special effects.

The grip has to move the lights in preparation for each scene.

The script supervisor watches all activities related to the correct use of the script.

The videotape recorder runs the machine that puts the film footage on tape.

The film or tape editor handles the raw footage and puts it together so that the film is ready for televising.

The title designer designs the program's title or logo.

The sales representative acts as liaison between the sponsor and the program's producer.

The advertising executive handles promotion for the program, including advertisements in newspapers, TV selection guides, and so forth.

The program schedule director is responsible for when each program goes on, both on a seasonal and daily basis. There is a great deal of psychological juggling involved here, as certain programs are selected as lead-ins to new or not-too-popular programs. For instance, established programs that are strong and widely viewed are scheduled ahead of a program the station wants to promote in the hope that the viewers will keep the set on and be "caught" by the new program.

The announcer's voice is heard at station breaks, or introducing a show's host.

The telecine operator runs the broadcasting machinery and is responsible for avoiding any "dead" time between programs.

There are also peripheral services that are involved in production. These include companies that design and manufacture television equipment, film manufacturers and film processing services, companies that handle storage and rental of produced films, and other organizations that manufacture film reels and cans.

There is still one more category of people involved in TV-related work. This includes journalists who concentrate on all aspects of television as it affects viewers: the editors and reporters who publish periodicals such as *TV Guide;* and the many TV reviewers whose columns appear in daily newspapers and magazines or who broadcast their comments on the radio and TV. The opinions of these writers carry a great deal of weight in whether or not a program, a series especially, is watched by enough viewers to earn a rating good enough for the sponsor to continue buying it.

Show Dissections

Show Dissections are divided into three levels from simple to more complex. You can select the kinds of activities that seem most appropriate for each of your children.

Decide before the program what specific parts everyone will watch to talk about afterwards. For those children who write with ease, suggest they make notes to refresh their memories later on. Plan to watch all or as much as possible of the same programs your children view.

The following suggestions are for things your children can spot. They are based primarily on situation-comedy programs, the ones best liked by children. They will also apply to many children's shows, such as those produced by Children's Television Workshop, that resemble magazines in format and contain short dramatic episodes.

Level One
* Describe everything you can think of about favorite characters.
* Think about why the characters are not people really being themselves but actors pretending just for the program.
* What happens to the characters?
* Do they act as real people and animals do?

Level Two
* Explain each character: age; type; appearance; personality; relationship to other characters. Are they like real people or animals? Describe some of the things the actors do that make them seem so much like people in real life. In what ways do they behave differently from actual people?
* Describe place(s) where the action occurs.
* Outline the plot: storyline; main and side themes; excitement; suspense; sadness; happiness; humor; etc.
* What are the problems? How are they handled?
* Is the show based on: what could happen to anyone; imagination; a combination of both?
* If you noticed, describe: sound effects; music; lighting; any special effects.

Level Three
* Analyze each character: believable; imaginative; exaggerated; likeable; in "bad guy" or "good guy" role?
* Describe where the action occurs. Do the sets seem realistic or not?
* Is the overall treatment of the characters, settings, and action: exaggerated; simple; glamorous; frightening; imaginative; believable; or what?
* Outline the plot: how is the viewer introduced to the story line? Does the main theme unfold clearly? Are there subplots woven throughout? Is it easy to foretell the ending, or is the plot complicated? What is the pace: slow, fast; mixed?
* Follow the plot rhythm flow from its introduction, before and after commerical breaks, to the ending. When do the peak moments occur?
* Problem solutions: what were the main problems? Did they seem realistic; exaggerated; unusual, but probable; silly? How were the problems handled: realistically; too easily; unwisely; sensibly? Would you have tried to solve the problems differently? If so, how?
* Rate the show: immediately afterwards; the next day; the next week. Use this scale: excellent; good; fair; poor; bad. State reasons for any change of opinion. Compare the show to others: in the same series; similar programs; specials.

- Describe the kind of mood(s) established: scary; funny; silly; slapstick; romantic; sad, exciting, suspenseful. How are the moods built up: music, lighting; sound effects; dialogue; silent action; laughter in background (live audience or canned?); scenic shots; buildup of action; fast-paced or noisy action; closeups of faces; "magic" and/or dramatic effects?

Pretend Production Planning

Turn your family into a TV production company's board of directors. Maybe you could call your company "TV Turn On Productions" or "Our Family Products." Encourage the children to do most of the planning, and decide on the following:

Type of program: series or specials; comedies, dramas, or
    documentaries
Age range of audience
Main kind of message to be emphasized
Length of program: half or one hour
Kinds of topics: typical family situations; fantasy; based on
    favorite stories; famous people; and so forth
Program format
General tone: serious; light; humorous
Size of cast
Time setting: now; long ago; imaginary age
Special effects: music; lighting; "magic"
Type of sponsor or actual sponsor preferred

As you go along, the family will probably come up with more and more ideas. Make Pretend Production Planning a long-range family game. It might even be interesting to keep a brief written account of your plans so that you can add to and compare your different ideas.

Network Programming

This project is an extended combination of the preceding two. For this, have the family don the imaginary hats of top network executives who are responsible for selecting the next season's programs from several pilot shows. Since the activity requires viewing several different prorams of the same type, it is a good way to get your family to try shows they have never before seen. The main caution here is that you closely monitor what they select to be certain they don't turn on a program of which you disapprove.

- Decide on how many and what kinds of the various types of programs are appropriate: situation comedies; documentaries; sports programs; scientific programs, including specials such as *National Geographic;* talk shows; game shows; news programs, historical dramatizations; interview programs; instructional programs such as *Gardening from the Ground Up;* music programs; dance programs; review programs; and so forth.
- Detail criteria for the programs: the kinds of things that you want included; specific things to be avoided.
- Ask at least two family members to watch at least two different examples of each kind of program. Compare and rate these, getting a consensus of opinion as to which ones are to be selected.
- Review all the programs chosen to be sure there is a good balance among them. Plan a weekly time schedule including all of the programs you have selected. Keep in mind the ages of the viewers so that programs most suitable for the youngest children are on the earliest in the evening.
- Select appropriate sponsors for each program. Don't necessarily choose actual sponsors, but find those whose products and services you consider are beneficial, trustworthy, and suitable for family audiences.

Script Writers' Symposium

Script Writers' Symposium offers your family many opportunities to pool creative and imaginative ideas. Once you suggest the outline of the procedure, you probably won't have to do much more than sit back and enjoy listening to what they work out. Before starting, it might be a good idea to arrange for someone to jot down some of the main points raised so that none will be lost in the general hubbub; ones discarded now might prove useful for future projects.

This is how to proceed: Pretend that you are a team of free-lance script writers who have been asked to submit an outline for a television series. This should include a fairly detailed script for the opening show, or pilot.

- Brainstorm for a general theme. This could be almost anything: *How to Avoid Family Fights; If Children Ruled the World;* or *What If There Were No Schools?*

- Decide on the main and secondary characters and make up detailed descriptions of each; will they be real or imaginary?
- Discuss all aspects of the setting: place; era; time of year; indoors or out, or both; or different sets for each situation.
- Outline the action for at least thirteen shows, including the pilot.
- Make up a detailed description of the pilot, breaking up the action into scenes. Try to keep the scenario as clear as possible. Try for a surprise ending.

Commercial Productions

TLC (tender loving care) Commercial Productions is a combined learning and experimenting activity. Its main purpose is to open the children's eyes and minds to the forceful impact of commercials by having them become aware of the devices used: slickness; polish; sensationalism; glamor; catchy music, voiceovers, sound effects; exaggeration; repetition; a fast pace; glossed over, souped up, half-truths; and other tricks that make most commercials so deceptive. When introducing this activity, the first thing to do is to study commercials with your family and help them pinpoint techniques such as those listed above. Once they have become more discerning commercial viewers, they can try the following activities:

- For warm-ups, suggest that the children change some of the commercials with which they are most familiar. Ask them to tell you what their changes signify, if they have any particular reason for them other than just the fun of attempting them.
- Plan for the creation of original commercials. This can be done as a family project or individually. Be available to offer any assistance that might be needed if the children work independently on this.

  - Select some favorite toy, food, book, game, place, idea, or whatever.
  - Decide on the most important features or points to include in a TV advertisement for the selection.
  - Make a Story Board for the ad. This should include the script and the visuals, or illustrations. For similarity to actual Story Boards, also include directions for the camera, lighting, sound and special effects, voiceovers, musical background (perhaps the child can choose a tune of a familiar song), logo or insignia, and whatever other details are noticed in commercials.

Teddy Bears	GLOSSARY	Page 1

LS-Long Shot   C-Cut D-Dissolve H-Hold
MS-Medium Shot P-Pan CU-Close Up
  FI-Fade In   FO-Fade Out

CAMERA	VISUAL	SCRIPT
From LS, with gradual P to final CU of bears face.		Teddy Bears bring happiness!
LS		Teddy Bears are always there.
MS	OXO	To hold, to love, to kiss.
LS		You can take them anywhere.
CU D		They're nice to have to hug.
LS		Put them by you at TV.
CU		Read them your favorite books.

Sample Story Board

Teddy Bears		Page 2
CAMERA	VISUAL	SCRIPT
CU		They can hold the books, you'll see.
MS		Or serve as handy clothes hooks!
MS		Bears come in all shapes and sizes.
MS		They can be soft, hard or squishy.
LS		If you don't have a bear, make one.
CU		Paper bag bears are hugable, too!
From LS, with gradual P to final CU of bears face.		Teddy bears bring happiness. Get one!

T. L. C.

COMMERCIAL PRODUCTIONS   4/4/79

Sample Story Board

Funny, Funnier, Funniest

The main objective of this kind of view of television is to help children realize that a great deal of the humor we witness on TV is exploitive, not really funny. Often we laugh because we cannot avoid doing so; an incident rapidly presented with elements of surprise can seem laughable as it occurs. In retrospect it may seem to have tragic overtones, however. Much of TV humor consists of slapstick behavior, pratfalls, wisecracks, or put-downs that make the victims appear stupid or excessively naive. Worse still, sometimes terrible things happen to the butt of a joke, and the audience finds itself still chortling as the character is pronounced dead, or carted off to an ambulance.

Funny, Funnier, Funniest is designed to help the family learn more about how humor is produced and used on TV. Even though adults and children have different kinds of humor funny bones, Funny, Funnier, Funniest can work as a family project because it requires analysis more than value judgments.

- Watch comedy shows to determine what kinds of humor (slapstick, exaggeration, caricature, satire, repetition, pratfalls, innuendo, play-on-words) are used.
- On programs with laugh tracks, decide if the background laughter has any influence on your reactions.
- Make up your own version of a comedy program you usually see. Try to think of ways you could change or improve upon the funny parts.
- Keep track of the number and types of humorous scenes in your favorite situation comedies. If possible, count the number of times you laughed hard, snickered, or smiled. If you prepare individual charts ahead of time with headings such as Big Laugh, Continuous Laughter, Giggle, Smile, all you have to do is put a check mark in the appropriate column. Afterwards you can compare charts.
- Collect samples of humor from other sources such as comic strips, cartoons, columns in magazines or newspapers, books, or from funny things that have happened to your family. Talk about these and compare them to television humor.

The more children study everything they see on television, the more discerning viewers they become. Participation in activities based on production and TV-related occupations is an interesting way for them to learn many useful mass-media skills.

The next chapter describes activities inspired by television that will enable children to try out their own ingenuity and creativity.

Creative
Extensions of TV

9

When we watch the entertainment programs and the commercials on television, our eyes and ears feast on a banquet of creativity. It is all there for the taking, and this is just what we do. But it isn't necessary to get stuck in the role of spectators. There are many things you can introduce to your children that will start them off on creative tangents of their own. As long as TV is such a gold mine of ingenuity and artistic delights, you might as well use it to summon your own muses to your sides.

There is a very good reason for promoting the use of imagination and creative talents. Everybody agrees that people can stay in better mental health by expressing themselves through some kind of creative outlet. It doesn't matter what is done as long as it stimulates feeling, thinking, and doing. Creativity takes many forms, from cooking an unusual and original casserole to painting the *Mona Lisa*. In contemporary phraseology, creativity is "doing your own thing." Try to get everyone in your family in the habit of doing their own things, yourselves included. Not only will everyone enjoy themselves, but hopefully the time spent on their own creative production lines will replace some customary TV time. What more could you want?

Join me now on a brief fantasy trip that I trust will turn into reality. Picture your family busily and happily occupied, everyone tapping their own potentials for planning and completing an original project. The TV set stands cold and dark. Your children are excited about what they are doing rather than about what is being done to them. Their creative juices are working. Away they soar, free of TV's spell!

However, we must be aware that not all children will show enthusiasm at first for doing something original. If they are not accustomed to this kind of self-propelled activity, they might be reluctant to attempt it. They will probably demur, claiming that they don't know how to do anything, or that they have no ideas. You may have to use a lot of patience and tact to get them started, without seeming pushy or overbearing. Try not to become too discouraged, however; even meager results are worth the struggle. The attempt to help your children discover themselves and some of their own abilities is a gamble that can have long-range benefits as well as more immediate ones.

Sometimes undertakings such as this are more successful if a definite time is set aside for them. Before involving the children, decide how much time you have and the most convenient hour for you. Of course the more time you can set aside the better, but even a small segment, such as fifteen minutes, might work. Within a fifteen-minute period you can at least get the children started each day. Be thoughtful about the most appropriate time for the children, too. A project such as this should not interfere with opportunities for active play with other children.

Once you are satisfied with the time part of the plan, go to the family and tell them what you have in mind. Explain that you would like to set up a family club for doing all kinds of "artistic" projects. Even if the initial reaction to this is negative, insist that everyone give it a try. Start them thinking about and discussing this idea immediately. Brainstorm for a club name, suggesting examples such as Momkid Club, Ridkidvid Hours, NTV (No TV) Time, or Our Hour.

Mention that you are making a time commitment to the club and that you will be available for a portion of all meetings and will try your best to be nearby during the rest of the time. Offer whatever other inducements you can, such as telling them they can invite friends to meetings once the club is launched, or that you will have surprise snacks for the meetings.

Suggest a reward system for their participation if you feel it is necessary to get them interested. I admit that this is a bribe, but with some children it is the only method that works, particularly at the outset. Once the children start cooperating, chances are that they will become intrigued enough with the club to persevere with fewer and fewer external rewards. Talk about the rewards ahead of time. Try to make them as special as you can, such as visits to away-from-home places, cook-outs, overnight camping trips, or whatever pleases your family the most.

Encourage the children to think up as many ideas as they can for the club. Tell them that even though you will definitely be a part of it and will be doing some creative things yourself (if you are sure you will, and I urge you to for your own pleasure), you want this to be *their* club with you gradually taking on the role of consultant, not chief promoter.

Here are some preliminary things you and the children can do to prepare for and get the club into action:

* Decide where the club will meet. If you are unable to leave its trappings set up on a permanent basis, make portable storage and work units out of grocery cartons, attaché cases or briefcases, small canvas suitcases, tote bags, or knitting bags with flexible stand-up frames.
* Arrange for a display area for artwork. This can be a shelf, or part of one; an end table; part of a larger table; a bulletin board; the back of a door; a large portfolio (commercial or made of large pieces of heavy cardboard and tied with strong ribbon or fabric strands); an easel; the refrigerator; or, for light objects, a homemade mobile.

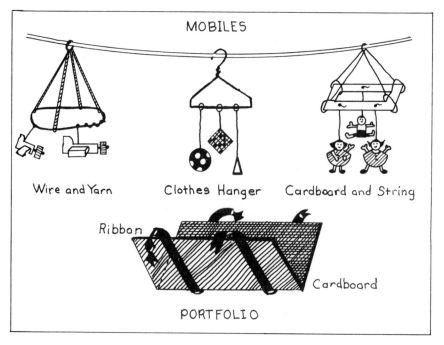

Ways To Display Artwork

* Set up a record-keeping system for Planned Projects, Projects in Process, and Future Projects. Although these sound rather formal, they can motivate the children to complete what they start as well as serve as reminders for interesting ideas not yet tried. These can be very simple charts. Post them in a prominent spot, easily noticeable.

PROJECTS		
PLANNED	IN PROGRESS	FUTURE
Scripts 1 and 2 Joe and Ann	Script 1 Joe and Ann	Sets 1 and 2 Nancy and Mike
Reviews (new) Mike	Reviews (dd) Mike	Travelogue Everyone
Mini dolls Mom Ann Nancy	Mini dolls Mom Ann Nancy	Plant Care Documentary Everyone

Sample Project Records

• Assemble the materials you think will be needed at the beginning. Put these in a special place and label them For Club Use Only. Make a firm rule that these things cannot be borrowed for other uses without the consent of all club members. This is the only way to prevent things from getting mislaid. The variety of things you might possibly use is endless, so the following list is only a partial one. You may find that you have to ask relatives, friends, and neighbors to help you with your collection.

pencils	hole puncher	paper (all kinds)	material scraps
felt pens	scissors	yarn	nails
crayons	tape	ribbon	buttons
erasers	glue or paste	string	toothpicks
clips	boxes	catalogues	pipe cleaners
poster paint	styrofoam	newspaper	bags
cartons	magazines	ruler	clothes pins
stapler	notebook rings	clear contact paper	wire hangers

Refer to Chapter 10 for suggestions about workspace, materials, and cleanup.

- Describe the club to those people who help care for your children, such as sitters and grandparents. Encourage them to interest the children in club activities when they are responsible for your children.
- Make up a supplementary portable supply box that the children can take along on visits to other people's houses, grandparents' especially.
- When the children are working on a project, give them guidance when they request it, but *do not do things for them.* Allow them independence in their creative efforts.
- Be accepting of the children's products. Do not set unrealistic standards for what they can achieve. Offer only constructive criticism, such as "That will probably stay together better if you glue it." Remember, you want the children to feel and become competent. Respect their efforts and achievements no matter how inept they are.
- Don't compare a child's products with those of others. Stress each person's uniqueness.
- As much as you can, do projects of your own, but be careful not to make them identical with what the children are attempting. Your adult expertise could easily discourage the children from trying things themselves.

As the following activities are not age graded, you will have to adapt them to suit individual children's capabilities. For ways to do this, you might find it useful to review Show Dissections in Chapter 8. It always takes some trial and error to discover a child's performance and understanding levels; therefore plan to experiment to determine them. It is advisable to start by introducing relatively simple ideas. You can always upgrade them, and it is less risky to undershoot a child's capabilities than to overshoot.

Decide in advance to allow the children leeway in their own adaptations of the activities. They may want to take off in entirely different directions than those presented here. That is all to the good. In fact, the things they plan themselves may be much more meaningful and rewarding to them. Once you have motivated them, relax and relish their independence. Continue to show strong interest, however, in everything they do. They will appreciate your caring.

HELPFUL THINGS TO DO

Production Specialists

There are similarities in these creative activities to some of the suggestions made in Chapter 8. The ones presented here, however, are more detailed.

Scripts.   These can be written or dictated. Begin by asking the child to tell several episodes of a favorite show to get a feel for the story line. Note the following:

- type of situations
- how introduced
- scene changes
- crisis; denouement
- solutions; finales
- interplay of characters

• Ask the child to watch for shooting techniques:

- action: segmented; flowing; varied; drawn out
- type of shots: closeup; medium; long
- sound: silence; talk; sound effects; music; narrator

• Suggest that the child make up new endings and/or new segments to shows already seen. Scripts can be based on:

- the child's original ideas
- the child's own experiences
- someone the child knows well (pets, too!)
- fantasies such as "If I could be *anyone*" or "If I could go *anywhere*"
- the child's favorite stories
- ideas gotten from looking at a picture

Professional Scripts.   These might be fun for older children. Use the format shown for Story Boards in Chapter 8, but instead of using drawings in the "Visuals" column, have the child describe the action.

Script Timing.   This is difficult, but some children might enjoy it. Suggest the childen playact scenes they have written, and time how long the scenes take. Mention to them that overlong scenes are sometimes boring and lessen the dramatic effect.

Public Service Announcements.   Help the children spot these at station breaks. Talk about the meaning of these PSAs. Then ask the children to prepare some, using causes about which they feel strongly. There are several ways to do them:

Story Boards—see the sample in Chapter 8
Posters
Pamphlets—only a few pages

Set Designing.   Suggest that the children design sets for the scripts they are writing, make up new ones for their favorite shows, or create imaginary ones. Set designing can be done with:

- Drawings or Collâge Pictures—For the latter, use catalogues and magazines. The cut-out pictures can be pasted on heavy paper or cardboard.
- Three-dimensional Mini-Sets—Small boxes can be glued, taped, or stapled on cardboard "floors" that are placed in a larger, shallow box with three sides left intact for walls; the fourth side is cut out of the front. Try to get outdated swatches from upholstery, carpet and floor covering, and wallpaper stores for set decorating.

Sample Cardboard Box Mini-set

Life-Scale Sets.   If you have extra space in your house or garage, help the children collect furniture and props to arrange sets there. A slightly smaller version of this is to get a big cardboard carton from a large appliance store, cut out one side, place the carton on its side, and let the children design their set inside.

Props.   Again, help the children collect these. Be careful not to give them *carte blanche* for this, however, as in their enthusiasm they might select some of your more precious and fragile objects. Whenever possible, encourage them to improvise props using junk materials.

Costumes.   Suggest that the children create costumes by mixing up clothes and accessories, something they enjoy doing; or by designing and actually making costumes, which is much harder. There are several choices for how to make them:

- Paper costumes can be made out of large extra-strong bags or wrapping paper. They can be stapled, taped, or loosely basted together. After they are assembled, it is easy to decorate them with crayons, felt pens, paint, collaged paper, or material scraps.
- Material remnants can be draped and held together with belts, ribbons, or pins, or can be loosely basted.
- More substantial costumes will take more time and effort, so it is wise to make paper patterns for them. The children might even have fun drawing designs as a first step, then adapting the designs to the patterns before cutting the material.

Characters.   Even though the children and possibly you will be doing the acting, there may be a need for additional "actors." You can use the Supercolossal Rag Doll described in Chapter 6. Or if mini-sets are being used, you can help the children make small figures out of paper, tongue depressors, corks, old wooden clothespins, plastic bottles, twigs, sticks, chopsticks, styrofoam, tennis balls, and so forth.

Sample Mini-Dolls

Miniature Stages.   These can be made from large boxes, as described under Set Designing. Curtains, even paper ones, are a must. You can also improvise stages by covering a table with a large piece of material that can be draped, pinned, or tied back when the show starts.

Production Potpourri

There are a variety of different kinds of programs, based on those produced currently, that you can suggest to your children.

Travelogue.   Ask the child to select a favorite place away from home. If you have any pictures or postcards of the place, let the child use them. Suggest that the child write a script, make a story board, or draw a picture of the proposed Travelogue, using the following guidelines:

- description of the place and its surroundings
- how to get there
- detailed descriptions of the most outstanding features
- description of the people, what kind of houses they live in, how they earn their livings, and so forth
- how the place differs from home
- what, if any, animals live there; the kind of foliage
- unusual things one can do there

Documentary.   The child can select something familiar, such as a pet or favorite sport. Ask the child to think about the most important interesting points of the subject. Next suggest that the child write a script or draw a picture story as outlined above. A trip to the library to do "research" on the chosen subject might make this a more exciting project.

Docudramas.   Explain that these are dramatized versions of actual happenings, or history. To help the child get started, suggest events from your own family history, such as the day you brought the child home from the hospital as a newborn, or the child's first week in school, or a family camp-out. The Docudramas can be acted out spontaneously, or prepared with scripts or story boards.

Quizz Shows.   These can be more fun if the family is divided into Quizz Show master of ceremonies and participants, taking turns for these roles. You might even give the show a name, such as *Ridiculous Riddles* or *Who Are We?* The show can be done spontaneously, but if there is some preparation in advance it will hold people's interest longer. Prizes can run the gamut from extra-special hugs to not having to help with the supper dishes!

Song and Dance Extravaganza.   Based on musical reviews, this kind of show might be fun for the children to prepare for a large family party. Costumes and the use of make-up will probably be as exciting as deciding on what kinds of songs, dances, and comedy scenes to act out.

Cartoons.   If the children like to draw, they will enjoy doing these. Explain that cartoons are made up of many pictures, each one drawn to show one segment of movement. Suggest that the children try to follow this style, drawing as many pictures as they can. They can even effect the illusion of movement by flipping the completed drawings very rapidly; therefore the more they have, the better. Caution them to keep the drawings relatively simple so that they won't get tired of having to repeat too many details. Felt pens or thick crayons work well for this kind of art work.

Show Insignia or Trademark.   Ask the children to study these on the programs they watch. Then suggest that they make up new ones for those shows, or design ones for their own.

Sample Trademarks

Talk Show.   Try to find a fast-paced talk program in which the interviewer and participants seem to be enjoying themselves, such as the *Dinah* show. Watch with your children, discussing the different techniques used by the interviewer. Suggest that each child think up someone, real or imaginary, to interview. It might be easiest to start with a family member or friend. Ask the child to decide what aspects of that person's personality, experiences, or life might be of interest and to make up questions for the interview. Next, help the child outline segments of the interview:

- introduction to audience
- greeting to person
- questions
- summary and conclusion
- thank you to person
- goodbye to audience

Suggest that the children set up a place for the interview, selecting appropriate pieces of furniture, background, etc. Once this is organized, each child can enact an interview, with you and the rest of the family as audience. If it is difficult to have a real person to interview, use a pretend person as suggestd for Host a Favorite Character, with the child supplying the voice. Afterwards ask the child to critique the interview with you, working out possible ways to improve on the questions and style used.

Newscast or Sportscast.   Follow the same process as for the Talk Show by watching several different programs of this type with your children, talking over what happens. Let them decide which kind to start with. It might be fun and easiest to begin with family news, or a backyard baseball game. If necessary, help each child make an outline ahead of time for the information to be included in the broadcast. To make the show more interesting, the children can make drawings to illustrate some of the high points of the broadcast. Encourage your family to plan broadcasts on a regular basis, including the adults, too, as broadcasters.

Weathercast.   This is a variation of the activity above. For this you may want to get a portable chalk board or improvise an easel with large sheets of newsprint on which the children can draw the weather map during the weather broadcast.

How-To-Do-It Show.   If your children are not familiar with this kind of program, find one, such as *Gardening from the Ground Up* or *The*

Draw Man, to watch together. Let them decide what kind of specialists to be, either choosing a hobby or sport, or attempting something different such as *What Children Like Best—A Show for Parents* or *How to Be a Better Parent from a Child's Viewpoint* or *Way-Out Recipes.* The more imaginative the program, the more enthusiastic the children are apt to be. Do whatever you can to help each child plan a program and gather whatever display items or props are necessary. Again, this kind of activity is for every family member. It might even prove to be an eye-opener, showing how people feel, what they like, what they wish could happen.

Other People. This could be a mini-anthropological study of people who are different. If you know anyone whose background is different from yours, suggest that the children plan to interview them to discover any unique customs they have, noting as well the things they do that are like what you do. Help the children get started on plans for a program that covers some of these. You might even want to visit neighborhoods of people who are different, eat at their restaurants, buy some of their special foods, and try to cook as they do. Borrowing records of ethnic music from the library or from friends might make the program even more authentic.

TV Review. This is an activity that can become a very important learning experience for the whole family. Try to encourage everyone to participate. If the childen are too young to write, they can either dictate their reviews to you, or they could record them on tape. If all that seems too time consuming to you, a lot can be accomplished if the children just talk about shows, preferably at the supper table when everyone can hear. As TV reviewers your children will be developing several skills: they will learn to look carefully at the shows; they will begin to discern and discriminate; they will have practice in putting their ideas into words.

Start by collecting many different previews and reviews of television programs. Read and discuss them with your children. Point out the general rules of journalism: that the reviewer try to be as objective and fair as possible, and that the reviewer adds "in my opinion" when stating personal reactions. Stress the need for constructive criticism as opposed to just panning something.

Next, ask each child to watch a familiar program and prepare a review of it. After that, encourage the children to watch a program they usually do not view (here is a chance for you to introduce them to the kind of shows you would like them to see). Ask them to prepare a collective review the first time; for additional shows, encourage each child to write or tell you a separate review. If the children are enthusiastic about this, you could suggest they start a regular magazine of reviews, or keep what they prepare in a notebook. The following guidelines might prove useful:

- Start with name of the program, date, time, station, actors and actresses.
- Include a brief outline of the program.
- Mention the good aspects.
- Note the questionable or unsuccessful parts, if any, and why they detracted from the show.
- Discuss the acting on an individual basis.
- Analyze the plot, dialogue, and pace of the show.
- Describe and critique the setting, costumes, lighting, etc.
- Describe the sound effects and/or musical background.
- Note anything unusual about the titles and credits.
- State reasons for recommending or not recommending the show.

Television offers unending take-off points parents can use to stimulate children's involvement in creative activities of all kinds. The enjoyment children get from these can lead them to completely original projects, some of which are outlined in the next two chapters.

Forget TV! Other Interesting Things to Do

It is not realistic to assume that children will forget TV unless they have something absorbing to replace it. In this and the next two chapters I introduce a variety of activities that children enjoy and that stimulate them to be creative in areas far afield from television. Opportunities to use these avenues for self-expression and ingenuity are powerful antidotes to dependence on TV as a way to spend leisure time. I hope that your family will plunge into them with fervor.

In this chapter, writing is stressed, with adaptable suggestions for nonwriters and nonreaders included. These activities are more free-flowing than those used before, requiring a great deal of originality. They provide excellent opportunities for children to experiment with new ideas and to use the creativity that lies close to the surface in all of them. You may find that it takes only a few suggestions to make them want to get started.

It is best to first do preliminary research to determine each child's "creativity level." This merely entails careful observation to discover under what conditions and how each does things in a different, nonconforming way. Everything is significant here, whether it is in using nonsense words, making up crazy riddles or fantasies, finding an unusual use of toys or games, performing variations on disco dances, and so forth. Use these clues to choose appropriate beginning activities. Children who enjoy playing with words will undoubtedly like the writing ideas. Those who are imaginative with toys may respond well to arts and crafts.

Whenever possible, try to dovetail creative projects with each child's favorite activity. Focus your attention on what seems to absorb the child the most, then talk together about creative extensions to see what you can plan. For example, if your child is intrigued with a specific sport, the organization of a scrapbook involves creativity in collecting pictures and articles; writing up original stories, such as "I *am* a Baseball Bat" or "Around the World on a Skateboard"; or making illustrations. Once such a scrapbook is begun, other ideas for it will come to mind.

Inviting a child's best friend is often just the ingredient needed to successfully launch creative projects, as some children function better when they have company to join them on a new venture. There is the chance, too, that if the visitor's interest in what you are suggesting is keener than your child's, the visitor will serve as a good model. Even though you run the risk of the children copying each other, this may not last too long if you tactfully encourage that each one do a different version.

Community resources can provide inspiration for creativity. Take advantage of them. A few of these are:

- Parks, beaches, public gardens, where children can look at nature more closely to describe it in poetry, or sketch it.
- Museums that are full of art that serves as models for children's work.
- Architecture of all kinds that show children the many ways to build.
- Libraries whose books offer endless creative stimulation.
- Scenic spots where beauty and panoramas introduce children to unusual sights and perspectives.
- Airports, railroad stations, and bus stations where a variety of sights and sounds spark off children's imaginations.
- Utilitarian structures, running the gamut from water towers and power stations to telephone poles, that expose children to mechanical creativity.

To sharpen your sensitivity to the creative adventures on which your children will be embarking, try the following Awareness Activity. It will help you appreciate your own creative experiences, revealing to you the many facets of the creative process.

AWARENESS ACTIVITY

Creative Test Flight

Set aside a segment of time, at least half an hour's worth, when you can work alone and without interruption. Plan to do something new, or a different version of something done before, keeping the project on a small scale. For example, you may want to write a short poem; conjure up the ingredients for an exotic recipe; or fashion a tiny "sculpture" out of an assortment of readily accessible materials such as corks, paper clips, toothpicks, ribbons, bits of cloth, aluminum foil, and so forth.

As much as you can, either while you work or immediately afterwards, think about how and what you did in the following areas:

- Selection of materials or words
- Decisions made, and how reached
- How you work: quickly, methodically, spasmodically, spontaneously, with or without preplans, etc.
- Evaluations, if any, or changes made before completion
- Level of concentration: completely absorbed, aware of distractions, resentful of distractions
- Verbalizations: talking, singing, humming, sighing
- Feelings: general attitude toward the project, awareness of limitations, satisfaction with expertise, awareness of any pressures such as time or difficult materials
- Physical status: tenseness, fatigue, energy
- Reaction to finished product: willing or unwilling to show it to others

This is an appropriate spot to urge you again to join your children on their projects by doing some of the same things along with them. Your working beside them, implying both your interest and enthusiasm, can provide a strong incentive to them. Not only will they enjoy your companionship, but they will place higher value on these shared experiences because *you* are devoting time, thought, and energy to them. This is an example of how attitudes are "caught, not taught"; your willingness to try your own creative abilities side by side with your children will lend importance and greater significance to everything they do.

As mentioned before, you have to be extremely careful not to discourage your children's less able attempts by outdoing them with your own skills. You can avoid this by not allowing yourself to get carried away with what you are doing to the extent that you ignore them. Talk over with them that you want to join them, but that you do not intend that they view your products as ones they should copy. Keep reminding them that grown-ups may be more capable because of longer experience but that children's work can be just as beautiful and ingenious, in a different way. Your encouragement and admiration of what they do can convince them of this.

Writing

In some respects writing may be a logical point of departure for creativity because its medium is language, with which children are already well versed.

The main "tool" required is to stretch the mind and imagination in search of innovative ideas and modes of expression that can be adapted to different kinds of writing. Most children are responsive to these types of experiences when they receive concrete suggestions to get them started; others rarely need incentives once they discover how gratifying writing can be.

The activities included here are relatively simple ones, based on what children are most familiar with and find easiest to attempt. Hopefully your family will acquire the writing habit after doing them. Although we have not intended these creative projects to be school related, undoubtedly they will help children's writing and reading abilities through practice in the translation and organization of thoughts into writing, then reading what was written.

HELPFUL THINGS TO DO

Creative Writing and Younger Children

Even if your children are still preschoolers, they can dictate creative writing pieces. I recommend this highly not only to motivate their creativity but also as excellent preparation for writing and reading. You can try many of the following suggestions, appropriately adapting them to each child's understanding and capabilities. For instance, Mini-Tales can be simplified to a character or two and a short plot consisting of just a few incidents. Settings, character descriptions, and endings can be dispensed with if including them seems to inhibit the child's spontaneity or dampen enthusiasm.

The business of writing down the younger children's writing efforts is time consuming, but such recorded excerpts prove to be indispensible learning devices for a variety of reasons. Their authors:

- Take pride and pleasure in what they have done.
- Gain self-confidence about their own originality and aptitude for creative writing.
- Are interested in having their own pieces read back to them. This usually leads to attempts to read them themselves.
- Learn to value both writing and reading as worthwhile.
- Understand early on that anything that is said can be written or printed. This concept is essential for children to recognize as a prerequisite to learning to read.

Recording Children's Dictation

Here are a few hints for taking dictation:

- Record what children say without criticisms or corrections. Their first creative writing is usually crude, but ordinarily it improves with age and practice. You run the risk of turning them away from this kind of activity if you tamper with their work; therefore it is best to accept it as is.
- Whenever possible, try to copy the dictated pieces on notebook or larger paper, leaving space for the child to draw or paste in pictures should he or she wish to do so.
- Get in the habit of using manuscript printing, as opposed to block printing, as this is what children are first taught in school. You may wish to refer to the manuscript printing charts, pages 100, 101.
- Date each piece and keep the collection in chronological order. It will be interesting to you and your child to go over these from time to time.
- Ask other family members, especially older children who can write, sitters, grandparents, etc., to encourage the young ones to dictate to them.
- If you own a tape recorder, occasionally use it to record the children's voices reciting their own work. This applies to the older children as well. Suggest they begin each segment with a date and a title. Be sure to write these down on the spool so that it is easy to locate them later on. If the children want to make drawings that go along with the recordings, it might be a good idea to establish a numbering system for tapes and the accompanying illustrations.

Books For Children's Creative Writing

There is something special about bound collections of children's creative writing. Binding what they do in book form lends greater significance to their work than if it were left on individual sheets, probably to be lost or forgotten. Each child can accumulate his or her own library, adding to it throughout childhood. The saving of children's literary output represents subtle affirmation of their own abilities and can be an incentive to them to continue writing and reading. Such original books on family bookshelves also serve as first readers for younger children, and if treated with care may even fill the same purpose for the authors' own children several decades in the future!

MANUSCRIPT HANDWRITING
CAPITAL LETTERS

MANUSCRIPT HANDWRITING
SMALL LETTERS

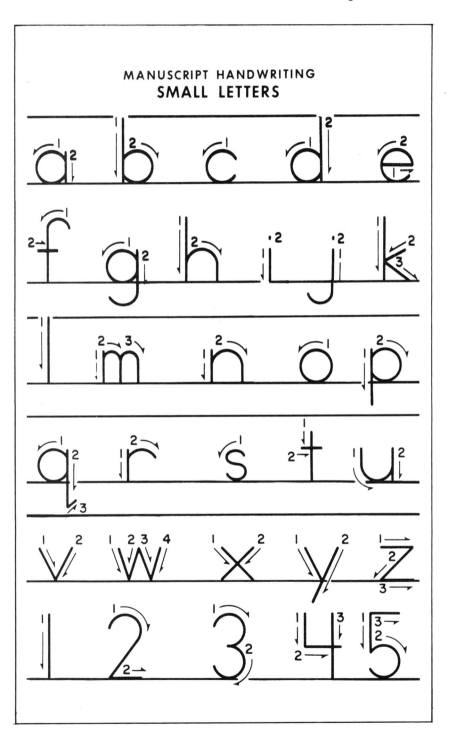

We strongly recommend making books for children of *all* ages. It is never too early to start this custom that for some children turns into a lifetime habit. There are several ways to do this, all of which the children can help with to a degree, depending on their ages. The very youngest can decorate the covers in some way; the older ones can do the entire process, with some guidance from you. In addition to commercial notebooks or scrapbooks, here are a few suggestions for homemade ones:

Soft-Cover Book

A Soft-Cover Book can be made by folding in half several sheets of paper, notebook sized or larger, and attaching them by:

- Stapling from the outside edge, then covering staples inside and outside with tape
- Sewing with thick thread and large basting stitches
- Tying with thick yarn
- Taping with library or masking tape
- Punching holes and using notebook rings

For durability, put contact paper on cover pages, both outside and inside, or make covers of heavy construction paper.

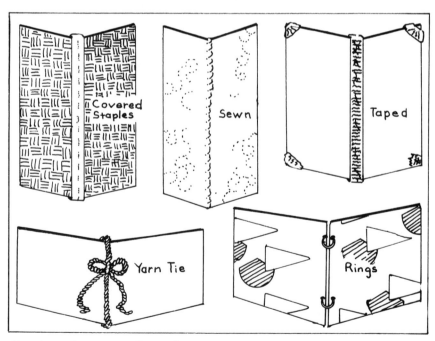

Soft-Cover Book Samples

Hard-Cover Book
You will need:

2 pieces of same-sized thick cardboard
Library or masking tape, at least 1'' wide
Paper sheets
Cover material—construction or contact paper, or some kind of fabric
Large needle and heavy thread
Paste, glue, or rubber cement

Cover. Join cardboards together with tape, leaving space between to fit in pages. Cut out the cover material, making the dimensions bigger than the cover's. Paste the material on cardboard, mitering the corners, starting first with the sides, then top and bottom.

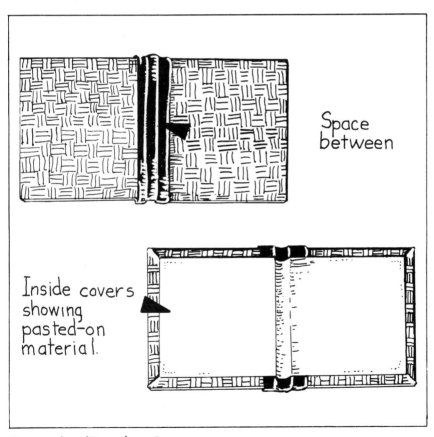

Space between

Inside covers showing pasted-on material.

Sample Book Cover

Pages.   Using five or six sheets at a time, fold them in half, then baste them together with big stitches, keeping the thread knot on the outside edge so that it will be hidden when pasted. Paste the first set of pages onto the inside of the book covers; add more sets of pages, one at a time, by putting paste on their spines, then setting them in the center-fold of the preceding set.

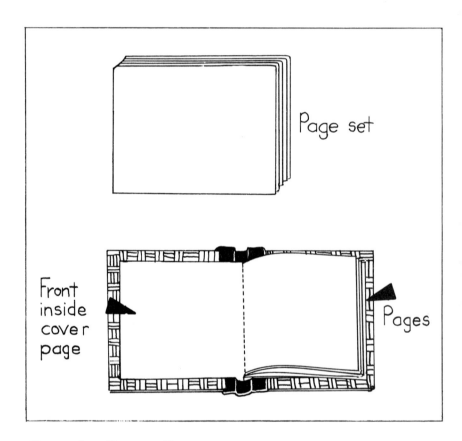

Page set

Front
inside
cover
page

Pages

Sample Page Insets

With every type of book, try to include the following details in imitation of actual books:

- On the cover, print the title and the author's name.
- On the spine, print the same information if there is room.

Sample Cover And Spine

- On the first, or title page, use the same information plus the date.
- Include a table of contents, numbering the book pages and giving the exact page location of each story, poem, or whatever.

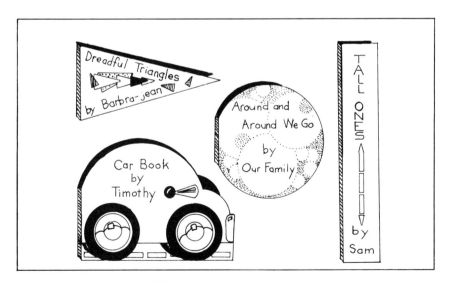

Sample Book Forms

I dare to guarantee that you and your family will be very satisfied with the results of your book manufacturing. You will be amazed at how attractive homemade books can be. It is hard to resist picking them up and reading them, no matter how simply constructed they are. Experiment with different sizes and shapes, too. There is no end to how appealing you can make these books.

What To Write

About Me

Generally children are not at a loss to describe themselves and what they like or dislike. They might enjoy the following, starting first with "word sketches" and working up to more detailed written pictures:

Self Portrait.   This can include a physical description plus an autobiographical account of the child's life to date.

Written Cartouche.   Explain that cartouches were used by ancient Egyptians to indicate people's names, enclosing hieroglyphics or symbols within an oval frame. For the Written Cartouche, the child can draw a large oval, divide it in half, then write one-word or short-phrase descriptions of himself or herself, perhaps putting physical facts on one side, other characteristics on the second side. Further on, I suggest a drawn version of this.

What I Like Best.   Ask your child to think and write about everything they enjoy, from people to food, from pastimes to favorite TV shows.

When I Am Bigger.   Your children's ideas of what they hope for themselves in the future may become more crystalized once they write them down.

My Life Two Years From Now.   Speculating on what they will be doing in the immediate future may reveal a mixture of your children's imagination and pragmatism.

Character Sketches

Children's keen powers of observation enable them to notice many details in others. There are several approaches you can suggest to get your child started:

The Funniest (Oldest, Most Beautiful, Busiest, etc.) Person I Know.   Once the child has decided on whom he or she wants to describe, the child should have no difficulty writing this kind of sketch.

A Storybook Character.   For this you can either read out loud or ask your child to read in order to find a character about whom the child would like to write more.

From Picture to Words. Ask your child to look at pictures in magazines, books, or photo albums to select people to describe in writing. *Made-Up People.* This requires more imagination than the other sketches, and your child might like to do this the most.

Biographies

It might be a good idea to get several biographies from the children's section in the library to give your child examples of this type of writing. Talk with the child about the different people, pets, or toys about which biographies can be written, like My Mother, Father, Grandparents, Aunts and Uncles, Cousins, My Favorite Friend (Teacher, Storybook Character), Our Dog (Cat, Guppies, Rabbit), My Teddy Bear (Doll, First Truck, Tennis Racket), and so forth.

Descriptive Passages

Tell your child to pretend he or she is a camera so that the child can write down everything he or she sees. Read some samples from favorite books of place or setting descriptions for inspiration. Here are some possible topics: My Room, The View From My Window, My School, An Airport Waiting Room, Our Hall Closet, My Toy Box, The Night Sky, Our Garden.

Happenings

Happenings are descriptions of events. Writing them so that they are clear and make sense is excellent practice for attempting more difficult short stories later. Ask your child to write either real or imaginary versions of topics such as: The Best/Worst/Shortest/Longest/Hottest/Coldest/Happiest/Saddest/Funniest or Strangest Day I Ever Spent.

For variation, read a provocative paragraph or page from a book and suggest that your child write an extension and ending to the situation. Or ask the child to write original beginnings and endings to familiar stories.

Imagination Voyages

Children do not have much difficulty taking off on these. Here are a variety of ways to set their imaginations whirling:

- Find some tiny objects to put in a small box or bowl. Tell your child to pretend to be a very small creature who discovers these, and to write up the creature's reactions.
- Suggest the child write one of these: Life as an Ant, Life on the Moon, If I Were a Giant, A Prehistoric Fossil Crab Comes to Life in Our Garden, If I Owned a Magic Wand, etc.

- Ask the child to sit quietly, relaxing as much as possible, and to close his or her eyes. Turn on some music, preferably without singing, and tell the child to listen until the music makes the child think of something original to write.
- Suggest your child use segments of dreams or nightmares to elongate into Imagination Voyages.

Mini-Tales

The preceding writing experiences were preparations for Mini-Tales, which are small short stories. To help your children tackle this harder writing form, I suggest as before that you read out loud or help find short stories for the children to read by themselves. Talk over how these are organized and their most important parts before the children attempt to write a Mini-Tale. A Mini-Tale should include the following:

- setting: time, place
- introduction of characters: main and secondary
- situation, or problems to be resolved
- plot line
- climax to which events have been building
- solution to problems
- ending

Mini-Tales in Tandem

If your children enjoy writing Mini-Tales, they may want to write them in serial form, using the same basic sets and characters but varying the situations. Another way to do this is to use a child's first Mini-Tale as the main event, then write separate tales, one for each character, describing in fuller detail what was happening to each of them just prior to their involvement.

Mini-Tales in tandem often turn into short novels. See if you can inspire your child to write one!

Plays

Writing plays is only slightly different from script writing, which was outlined in the previous chapter. Stage directions replace camera shots, but otherwise the same format is followed. Before your children attempt to write, they might enjoy using the Mini-Stage and Characters, described in the previous chapter, to work out the plot of the play.

Poetry

Children make fine poets as their fresh, unclichéd use of language lends itself to this kind of writing. Reading poetry out loud often sets children in the mood to try poetry composition; try to find poems to

read with your child. If you cannot find any, talk about the importance
of the rhythmical meter of the lines in a poem. Point out that not all
poetry has rhyming lines; often free verse or unrhymed poetry are also
effective.

Here are a few of the simpler poetic forms you can suggest:

Poetic Word Pictures are brief descriptions, broken into short lines.
For example:

The setting sun
Fills the sky with red,
Outlining cloud edges
With bright gold.

Triangular Poems take a form that appeals to children because of its
simplicity. It is written with one word in the first line, two in the second,
three in the third. It can be extended to result in a many-worded base.
Here is a short sample:

Bee
Buzz, buzz
Searches for honey

Cinquain Poems are more complicated than Triangular Poems but are
not too difficult for children. They are written this way:

Line 1—one word, the subject
Line 2—two words, adjectives describing the subject
Line 3—words that explain what subject is doing
Line 4—four to five words describing how the subject makes the
writer feel
Line 5—one word, a synonym for the subject

Here is a sample Cinquain:

Water
Clear, sparkling
Laps over my toes;
Makes me cool.
Waves.

Haiku Poems are based on an ancient Japanese style. This poetic form
is popular with children and is used frequently in schools. Traditional
Haiku are objective views of nature, usually including some words that

signify what season of the year it is. Each Haiku has seventeen syllables, broken up this way:

Line 1—5 syllables
Line 2—7 syllables
Line 3—5 syllables

Here is a sample Haiku:

Trees slowly shed leaves
As whistling winds whirl through them;
The forest turns gray.

Writing and Illustrating

In addition to illustrating the writing projects already suggested, there are other combinations of writing and drawing that children like to do. Here are several:

All-Occasion Cards.   Try to get your children into the habit of making greeting cards instead of buying them. You might even mark important events on the calendar, with warnings at least a week ahead of each one so that the card designers will be certain to get their work done on time. Children who particularly enjoy this kind of activity can be encouraged to produce large numbers of cards to make an ever-ready stockpile. With your approval, they might even sell cards. This could turn into business training for the more enterprising, especially if they use the money earned to defray the expenses of buying necessary supplies. They will learn quickly about profit and loss from such an experience!

Drawn Photo Album.   This is fun for children who are intrigued with drawings, which they can do in lieu of using a camera. Such an album consists of sketches of family, friends, favorite places, special occasions, scenery, imaginary creatures, or whatever interests the artist. Encourage your children to write up detailed descriptions for each illustration. Drawn Photo Albums can turn into fascinating books, worthy of display on the coffee table and to be treasured along with other family souvenirs.

Illustrated Journals.   These are ongoing illustrated records of what happens each week, a form of collective family diary. If a loose-leaf notebook is used, it is easier for everyone to add pages and keep them in chronological order. Ask each contributor to date each page. Even if you are not much of an artist, add your entries, too; you can always draw stick figures. Like Drawn Photo Albums, these journals are nice to keep, not only for nostalgia trips when the children are grown, but to use as reference for determining when certain events took place.

Once children get started on their own creativity, they become enthusiastic and prolific producers of many types of artistry. The self-confidence and feeling of accomplishment they gain from attempting their "own thing" serve as wedges to wean them away from TV. Go to the next chapter for more interesting projects in arts, crafts, music, and rhythms.

More Creative Replacements for TV

The number and diversity of things children can do in all of the arts are legion. It is hard to know where to *end* listing them. This chapter describes a potpourri of activities, dividing them loosely into categories of drawing and painting, sculpture, and music and rhythms.

Workspace

It is important that children have adequate room in which to work on artistic projects. You will also have to consider that long-range endeavors might necessitate leaving everything out, either to dry or to wait for next steps in a process. Be prepared for such contingencies by arranging for either a temporary or permanent "studio." This can be a card or improvised table in a corner of a porch, room, or hall, provided there is proper lighting; or tables or large boxes set up in a section of an attic, garage, service porch, or wherever you can comfortably fit in children and supplies.

HELPFUL THINGS TO DO

Artist's Work Table

As many children work well on the floor, determine if yours can before worrying about tables. Should they prefer a more raised work surface and if you are short on tables, either look for inexpensive plastic ones available in drug and large variety stores, or try building your own. You will need:

4 identical grocery cartons with lids still attached
Masking tape, as wide as you can find
A piece of heavy cardboard, fiberboard, or contact paper, cut to fit over the 4 boxes placed together to form a square

To build your table, tape the four boxes together and cover them.

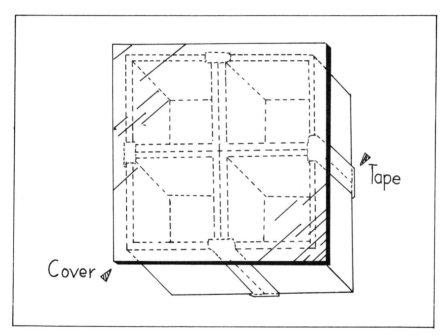

Tape

Cover

Sample Artist's Work Table

Chair Easel

A chair easel can also be simply constructed. For this you will need:

A folding or straight back chair; if you have a tall child, use a chair with arms to raise the level of the easel
An old blanket or large plastic sheet
A piece of heavy cardboard, composition board, or plywood, at least 24" by 24", to use as easel board
Tape

To build the easel, drape the blanket over the chair seat and legs. Place the board against the chair back. If it tends to slide, put several layers of heavy tape across the blanket, just in front of where the easel board should rest.

For paint-jar trays, use aluminum foil loaf pans, or shoe boxes split in half.

Attach paper to the easel board with clothes pins or large clips.

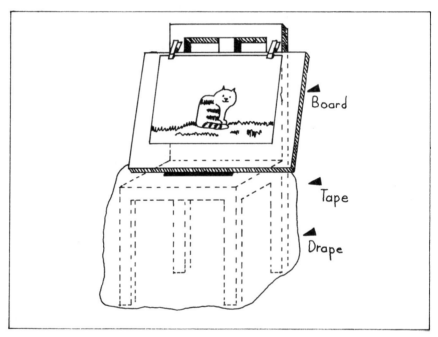

Sample Chair Easel

Easy-On Smocks

It is always wise to provide coveralls or smocks for the children to wear as many of the art materials, some paints especially, are hard to wash out of clothes. For those children who resist, see if they would be more amenable to a homemade Easy-on.

Weighted Easy-On

To make a weighted Easy-on smock, you will need:

Heavy plastic, or other durable material
Heavy dress weights, or dry beans

Cut the material to the child's measurements, leaving the straps long enough to hang to the middle of the child's back. Sew weights or beans, wrapped in cloth like a bean bag, onto the ends of straps to prevent them from slipping so that the smock will stay on. Add pockets.

Sample Weighted Easy-On

Permanent Tent Easy-On
To make a tent Easy-on, use heavy plastic or other material.   Fold the material, leaving enough in front to hang to the child's knees. Cut a hole for the head. Sew on pockets.

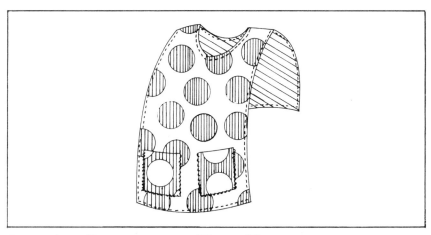

Sample Permanent Tent Easy-On

Disposable Tent Easy-On

To make a disposable tent Easy-on, use large grocery bags. Cut along the middle of one side of a bag. Cut along the middle of the bottom and the sides of the bottom. Turn the bag horizontally, with the uncut side on top. Refold the uncut side so that the bag is longer in front than in back. Cut the head hole out of the uncut side.

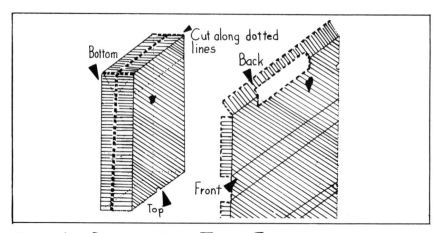

Sample Disposable Tent Easy-on

Clean-Up

Discuss clean-up rules in advance. Explain that you will be as lenient as you can about overlooking messes during a project, but that the children are responsible (offer your cooperation to the younger ones) for keeping everything as neat as possible at other times. Give them ideas to help establish a systematic way to arrange materials, using labelled grocery cartons, trays, baskets, plastic jars, and so on.

Materials

The selection of art materials and tools is not easy for nonartists. Although it is not necessary for children to have professional materials, it is wise to get good ones. Your best bet is to go to teachers' supply or hobby stores to make your purchases.

Here are a few hints to keep in mind:

- Large kindergarten pencils or those with soft lead are best for children's use.
- Buy wax crayons for preschoolers. Pencil crayons are appropriate for children about five or older.

- Look for nonindelible felt tip markers. Thin lined ones are not as satisfactory for younger children as the regular size.
- Library paste is excellent. You can also get dry paste, which is useful for big papier mâché projects. Look for the nontoxic kinds.
- Blunt-edged scissors are best for preschoolers. If one of your children is left-handed, ask for Lefty Scissors, which come both blunt- and sharp-edged styles.
- Clay comes in several varieties. We suggest moist clay that can be reused or left in the air to self-harden. It comes in 25-pound bags and can be kept indefinitely if wrapped in damp rags and placed in an airtight container.
- Look for pads of large (18″ by 24″) newsprint paper. Big paper like this is good for all ages, but most particularly for preschoolers who need broad areas when they draw and paint.
- Try to find *dry* poster paint as it is cheaper, longer lasting, and easy to prepare. It can always be thickened by adding liquid starch. If no dry paint is available, get tempera or liquid poster paint.
- Collected odds and ends from around the house or office, plus the other materials listed in Chapter 9 are essential accessories to the basic art materials you will have to buy.

HELPFUL THINGS TO DO

Drawing/Crayoning/Painting

Most art activities overlap in the use of materials for the creation of objects. Portraits, for instance, can be done in pencil, crayon, paint, collage, clay, styrofoam, or a mixture of many materials. Use our suggestions flexibly, therefore, and encourage your children to experiment with everything. The more extreme their combinations, the more creative pleasure they will have.

Portraits
As even small children like to draw people, introducing portraiture as a beginning activity will probably be appealing. The following different kinds of portraits can be used either for self-portraits or for portraits of other people.
Posed Portrait. Tell the child to sit in front of a mirror and try to do a realistic life-size picture of himself or herself. Some children may prefer to do the face and head only. For variation, you can suggest reducing the Posed Portraits to Miniatures.
Cartoon Self. Tell the child to exaggerate the self-portrait, making a caricature.

Jumbled Image.   This is an abstract, a la Picasso portrait, done with shapes, splashes of color, and distortions. After it is done, the artist can have fun testing the family's ability to identify eyes, nose, hands, etc.

Favorites Miniature.   Ask your child to make a small picture of his or her favorite possessions and pastimes, arranging them to create a symbolic picture of what the child values and does the most.

Mood Portraits.   Talk with your child about different moods, then suggest that the child express some of his or her own with separate Mood Portraits. Doing these can be effective safety-valves for bad moods, while those reflecting good moods may be worth hanging as reminders of happiness. If your child enjoys Mood Portraits and does a lot representing good moods, why not decorate a whole wall with them? Such a wall might be an incentive to turn bad moods into good ones!

Mixed-Media Portraits.   This type can be very attractive, especially if parts are done in collage, giving the portraits dimension.

Artistic Cartouche.   A Written Cartouche was suggested in Chapter 10. Now ask your child to draw things that could represent the child's name or personality, add other decorative symbols, and put them in a cartouche frame.

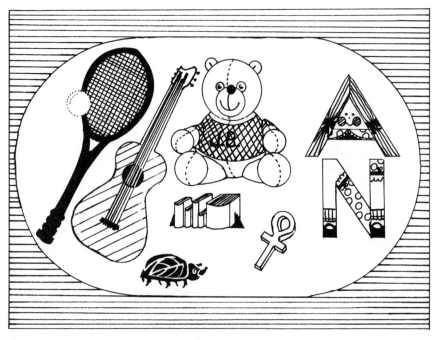

Sample Artistic Cartouche

Still Lifes

When they start to draw, many children do Still Lifes spontaneously. Therefore they will enjoy this art form with which they are already familiar. They like the challenge of formal arrangements, working on them hard and carefully.

Close Views are good for starters, requiring no special setup and using the surrounding environment as the focus point. Ask your child to get comfortably seated anywhere in the house, then look straight ahead, and make a Close View Still Life of what he or she sees. Caution the child to select a small segment of the scene so as not to be overwhelmed with too much to copy. To facilitate this, either you or the child can make an artist's viewer frame out of heavy paper or cardboard. The viewer is also useful for choosing an out-of-doors landscape. By holding it in front of the eyes, the artist can shift the viewer around to define the boundaries of the picture the artist wants to recreate.

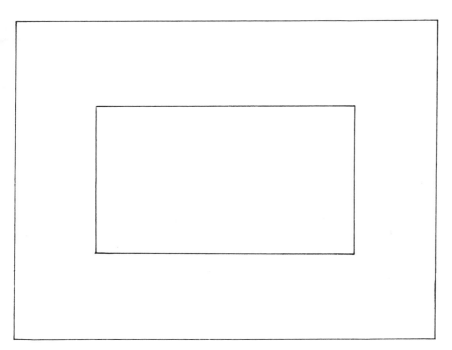

Sample Artist's Viewer

TV Screen Scene is a tricky version of Close Views, and it may not work unless your TV set is opposite a window that in daylight will throw on the screen a reflection of that part of the room that is in front of the set as well as the scenery outside the window! The resulting image is slightly wide-angled, as the screen is convex. The picture is fascinating, particularly because one finds oneself right in the middle of it. Use of the artist's viewer might be advisable here, too. It might do your heart good to see your child seated in front of a TV set without watching television!

Arrangements is a traditional kind of Still Life that offers childen the chance to select and artistically group objects as well as create pictures. For inspiration, it never hurts to show them Still Lifes from art books, ads in magazines, papers, or billboards. There are a great number of combinations of Arrangement Still Lifes. Here are some ideas:

- Favorite toys, books, possessions
- The most beautiful thing(s) in our house
- Family heirlooms
- Favorite fruits, houseplants, flowers
- Small things we use every day
- Potpourri of socks, ribbons, sofa pillows
- Jewelry treasure chest

The articles can be made more interesting to draw in several ways:

- Drawn from different angles, such as front, back, side, above, below (by putting them on a glass or clear plastic table or raised tray)
- Put against a reflecting mirror or a variety of backdrops
- Covered by unusual materials, such as netting, lightly colored clear plastic, mesh screening
- Drawn in bright or dull light; shadows; day, electric, or night lights

Landscapes

Prepare for taking spontaneous advantage of outdoor scenery too good to be missed by carrying in your car or picnic basket sketch pads, pencils, crayons, pastels, and a viewer. Taking photos of these scenes is helpful, too, especially if your children do not have time to finish their pictures while on the spot. Later on the photos will refresh their memories of what they saw.

Although nature scenes are most popular for Landscapes, here are additional suggestions for your outdoor artists:

- Marinas, harbors, bridges, railroad tracks and yard, city centers
- Large boulevards, highways, freeways, and interchanges, seen from a distance
- New road construction
- Plazas, squares, parks, sports arenas, outdoor theaters

- Farms: fields, buildings, equipment
- Views through the windows of your home: yard, garden, fire escapes, front stoops, adjacent buildings

Murals

Children's collaborative Murals are appearing more and more in public places like airports and civic buildings. They are always eyecatching with their freshness and color. You might want to "commission" your own children to make one or several to brighten up dull or empty wall spaces such as halls, game rooms, or garage interiors.

You will need large paper for this. Some teacher supply stores stock rolled paper and may sell you a partial roll. With luck you may be able to buy a small amount from your local newspaper or printer. If no rolled paper is available, make your own by taping together, on the wrong side, large newsprint paper. You can even use regular newspaper sheets, which make an interesting background for Murals.

I suggest you clear floor space for this project, as it is easier for children to avoid drips when painting on a flat area than if the paper is on the wall. If only one child works on the Mural, be prepared for the child to be involved with it for quite a while. It is a *big* surface for one person to cover.

Here are a few ideas:

Theme Murals. These can commemorate special events; be picture maps of the different places your family has lived or traveled; be a horizontal "journal" of the different things your family did during the summer; show imaginary places and happenings.

Decorative Murals. Anything goes here, from rainbows to space ships! The more things attached that move in the breeze, the more intriguing the Mural. Encourage your children to use all their art materials and supplies for these.

Scroll Murals. Adapted from Oriental scrolls, these should be relatively thin and long. They do not necessarily have to be on as large a scale as customary Murals; small ones are very attractive. To make them more authentic, you can mount the Scroll bottom on a cardboard paper towel tube, a thick stick, or a dowel stick. The sticks act as weights when the Scrolls are hung and also are handy for rolling up unused ones. If your artists' Scroll production is greater than your wall space, the extra Scrolls can be rotated from time to time with those already on the walls.

Designing with Paint

The next five activities are experiments with paint. As most of them are quite messy, lead your artists to washable places (floors especially) to do them. It is also wise to provide a pail of water near their work area so that they can rid their hands (or feet!) of excess paint before touching anything after they have finished.

Children get a big kick out of this kind of art work. Their completed creations can be extremely pretty, too.

Finger and Foot Painting.   This is a favorite in preschools, but older children like to do it as well. The painting can be done on a slippery table surface, in a tray with ¼" to ¾" sides, or on a highly glazed paper such as ditto, gift, or butcher paper. To preserve work done on paper, lay it down flat to dry, then press with a lukewarm iron on the wrong side. The pictures can be framed, used to decorate cartons, used to wrap gifts, etc.

Fingerpaint can be bought or can be made at home with this recipe:

In a double boiler, dissolve ½ cup of cornstarch with 2 cups of boiling water, and stir. Allow the mixture to come to a boil again. When it is cool, it will thicken.

To make Fingerpainting on paper easier for the children, first drop a small amount of water on the table before putting down the paper. Then dribble some water over the paper, asking the children to spread it around before putting the paint on the paper.

Dribbling.   This can be done with brushes, thick yarn or string, funnels, discarded plastic medicine droppers, or anything else that can hold enough paint to permit it to drip onto the paper.

Roll a Picture.   For this activity a tray with sides is useful but not obligatory. The procedure is to put several dabs of different colored paint on various parts of the paper, then roll or trail through the paint some object such as a plastic hair roller, a ball, a marble, some yarn, a sponge, a rough-surfaced cork, an orange or lemon.

Butterfly Blots.   Fold a piece of paper in half. Paint or drip generous amounts of varied colors of paint on one side. Then place the clean side on the painted one to "print" the design. Open the paper and leave as is, or add to the design.

Tray Painting.   This is another way to "print" a picture. Put generous amounts of varied colors of either finger or regular paint in a tray. Swirl the tray around to mix them, then lightly place a piece of paper on top to pick up the design.

Crafty Paper.   There are several ways to prepare paper so that when it is painted on, the results are unusual. Here are some ideas:

- Cut paper in freeform shapes.
- Cut or tear holes in paper.
- Paste an abstract form or forms on paper.

- Lightly sprinkle water in a few spots so that paint will run in them.
- Wet paper and squeeze out excess moisture.
- Use textured paper such as toweling or napkins.
- Ask for discarded wall paper sample books at decorator or paint stores; the children can paint on the backs of this paper.
- Make textured paper by creasing or crumpling it, or briefly squeezing it (hard), or rubbing it over patterned objects such as screws, cheese graters, spoons, and so forth.

Crayon Creations

Aside from drawing and coloring, wax crayons can be used for other kinds of art projects. See how well your children like these.

Rubbings. Ask the children to peel the paper off the crayons. Then give them sheets of paper and set them loose, indoors or out, to make designs by rubbing over objects placed beneath the paper. Watch for how ingenious their selections are. Rubbing works on anything: coins, jewelry, door mats, corrugated cardboard, keys, rocks, wood grains, pine cones, and so on.

Etching requires preparation that even preschoolers can do. The purpose is to put two layers of solid crayoning on thick paper, construction paper, or cardboard. Suggest to the children to start on small sheets, then use larger ones when they feel more ambitious. Effective layering consists of a bright color for the first layer, then black on top. Next the children can use a toothpick, nut picker, nail file, or any other small sharp instrument to "etch" their designs.

Stained Glass is an activity that requires more of your supervision, particularly with younger children. The results are usually very spectacular, and are easily converted into gifts or gift paper.

You will need:

A crayon sharpener, or a dull knife for the older children
Waxed paper
A tepid iron
Miscellaneous items such as feathers, yarn bits, leaves, etc.

Ask the children to sharpen or shave the crayons until they each have at least ¼ cup of the shavings. Next, cut two pieces of wax paper to the desired size. The shavings and other materials can be arranged in a design on one sheet of paper, waxy side up. This is then covered with the other sheet, waxy side down on the materials. Weight the edges of the paper to prevent them from slipping when the iron is first applied. After part of the papers are set, the weight can be removed. Leave the iron on the paper just long enough for the two pieces to stick to each other.

These Stained Glass pieces are striking when framed with dark bands
of construction paper. They can hang by windows; be assembled into
mobiles; be wrapped around half-gallon or larger cartons to use as what-
not boxes or wastepaper baskets; attached to form a frieze along a wall;
and so forth.

Bookmarks are another way to use shavings.

You will need:

Plain color material scraps, cut in strips about 1″ by 10″
Shavings
Iron
Heavy brown paper to protect your iron and board

Place two sheets of brown paper on a work surface, such as the iron-
ing board, before the child starts. The shavings can be scattered along
the material strip either freeform or in a design (this is hard for the
younger children). Cover the designed strip with brown paper, and iron
until the color bleeds through the top paper. Presto, the bookmark is
made. If the material lends itself to fringing, suggest the child do this
afterwards.

Variations of this kind of work on larger material are table mats or
runners, or sofa pillow covers.

Sculpture

I use Sculpture as a generic term covering a wide range of manipulative activities that never fail to absorb children. These are fun to do,
many are relatively simple, and the end results of all of them are interesting to look at.

Collages.   I have mentioned Collages before, but we give them more
prominence here. A collage is not exactly Sculpture but certainly can be
categorized as an intermediary step between Sculpture and flat, one-
dimensional art. For the novice artist, Collage is very satisfying as it
gives a semblance of design once one thing is pasted on the paper. From
there on, and much to the delight of children trying it for the first time,
a Collage grows quickly and easily.

Collages can be made on paper; in box lids to become shadow boxes;
on box sides and lids as decorations; on styrofoam bases; on drawings;
on paintings; on wall paper; on aluminum foil (stapled on); on burlap
and other material.

Anything that can be pasted, tied, stapled, clipped, sewn, or woven
can be used for Collages.

Mosaiclike Collages seem to fascinate older children. These are structured designs, usually requiring many of one item, such as beans, and must be done with patient and careful pasting.

Nature Collages are especially nice. Before collecting for these, it is best to tell your children to pick up only what is lying on the ground, and not to take living things such as attached bark or leaves. In some states taking *anything* from the seashore or parks is against the law, so check on this before starting on collection trips.

Junk Sculpture

Junk Sculpture is really three-dimensional Collage. For it you need strong glue and lots of small things from around the house, plus expendable items such as jar and bottle lids; plastic bread fasteners; used envelopes (the ones with windows are most intriguing); can labels; and whatever else you can find. Spread these all out on a table and let the children start building their Sculptures.

Special-Materials Sculpture

There are several kinds of materials that lend themselves to freeform Sculpture.

Wood. Ask for scraps at lumber yards; woodworking and cabinet shops; furniture factories; building sites. Try to collect wooden spools, although plastic ones are useful if wooden ones are no longer available.

Cardboard. Save all boxes; corrugated and other cardboard pieces; old playing cards; business cards; postcards; etc.

Styrofoam. Save from packages you get. Ask for throw-aways from electrical appliance, drug, and variety stores. Buy interesting shapes in hobby shops.

Sculptures can be painted and/or varnished when they are finished to give them a polished look and add to their durability.

Clay, Playdough, Bakable Dough and Papier-Mâché

All of these are children's perennial favorites. Some children just like to use them without a thought to preserving the finished products; others are intent on saving what they make.

Usually commercial clay is self-hardening; be sure to carefully read the directions that come with it so that you understand how this process occurs. With both clay and bakable dough (see recipe below), caution the children to vigorously knead the material before shaping to eliminate possible air pockets. Warn them, too, about too-thin appendages that are apt to snap off once the substance dries.

It is a good idea to provide a clay board, made of anything hard, on which the sculptured piece can remain throughout the work and drying periods.

I am not enthusiastic about children using tools for sculpture, preferring that they enjoy the direct experience of touching, squeezing, molding, and shaping the materials with their hands. The following tools are useful, however: tongue depressors; small rolling pins (cylindrical wooden blocks are fine); plastic knives; tooth or nut picks for small details.

Playdough
To make playdough you will need:

2 cups flour
¼ cup of salt
water
food coloring
1 tspn. alum, a preservative, available at drug stores
2 tbspn. odorless cooking oil

Mix dry ingredients together. Gradually add cold water and oil, kneading constantly until dough becomes pliable and does not stick to fingers. For extra embellishment you might divide dough into four parts and add a few drops of different food coloring to each part, then knead to spread color.

If kept in an airtight container in the refrigerator, playdough will last for an indefinite period. Occasionally it requires some cooking oil and/or water to prevent it from becoming crumbly.

Your children will enjoy making the playdough, so be sure to get them in on the act. A word of warning, however; don't let anyone with open sores on their hands use it, as it will cause stinging!

Bakable Dough
To make bakable dough, you will need:

2 cups salt
1 cup flour
⅔ cup water

Mix ingredients in a pot or double boiler. Slowly simmer until the mixture thickens. After the dough is molded, it can be baked one hour at 200 degrees. When cool, objects can be painted.

Papier-Mâché
To make papier-mâché, you will need:

Newsprint or newspaper, or any other thin paper
Liquid Ivory, or detergent

Tear newspaper or newsprint into small pieces (enough to fill a tightly packed household pail, plus ¼ pail of extra pieces to be left dry). Add boiling water and several large squirts of liquid Ivory or detergent until newspaper is saturated. Mix well and soak overnight. Squeeze as much water out of the newspaper as possible and begin to mold. Give each child a board on which to work and leave the sculpture to dry.

Warn the children that as with clay, it is important to pack the mâché tightly together so that it will not break apart when dry.

After the children have molded the mâché to their liking, tell them to cover the finished product with the dry pieces of paper, using paste to make them adhere.

Allow the pieces to dry; this may take several days to a week, depending on the dampness of the climate. If the dried pieces look messy, tell the children to apply one or more layers of extra paper until they appear smoother. When dry, the pieces can be sandpapered for smoothness, and painted and varnished.

Music and Rhythms

Music and rhythms are excellent balms for the TV-filled soul. They cast a kind of spell over people, at the same time both relaxing and freeing them to be more expansive and self-expressive. As a background for creativity there is nothing quite like music; it lifts and inspires, as well as pleases.

Before going any further I need to define the type of music and rhythms that this section covers. By *music* I mean *any* kind that appeals and makes the children want to listen and/or move to it. The same with *rhythms;* some of these I shall suggest will be extremely simple, but rhythms notwithstanding. What I hope will happen is that your children's appreciation for music and movement will increase, becoming a well-entrenched lifetime habit. With your guidance, it is possible for them to realize the many gifts offered by music, its ability to soothe, inspire, and enrich being the most rewarding.

If you own a phonograph or cassette player, the purchase of special children's records or cassette tapes will help. It is not absolutely necessary to buy these; however, I am sure both your family and you will like them. They are available in teacher's supply, better toy, and large record stores. Many public libraries circulate them as well.

The number of good children's records is so great that it is impossible to include them all. My short list is applicable mainly to my suggested activities in this section. Selections for younger children are on top, for the older ones on the bottom in each category:

Music for Listening
The Small Listener—Bowmar
Nature and Make Believe—Bowmar
Seagulls—Hap Palmer

Music for Movement/Dance
Pretend—Hap Palmer
Movin'—Hap Palmer
Rhythms of Childhood—Ella Jenkins

Activity Songs
The Small Singer # 1 & #2—Bowmar
Learning Basic Skills through Music, Vol. 2—Hap Palmer
You'll Sing a Song—Ella Jenkins

Folk Songs
Folk Songs for Little Singers—Bowmar
American Folk Songs for Children—Mike and Peggy Seeger
Songs and Rhythms from Near and Far—Ella Jenkins

Rhythms Orchestra
The Small Player—Bowmar
Homemade Band—Hap Palmer
This Is Rhythm—Ella Jenkins

Art To Music
As a transition from the activities in the preceeding section, we suggest this combination of art and music. Ask each child to gather material for the type of art work he or she likes best. Plan to join in as this will be enjoyable for you, too. After everyone is settled and ready to start, turn on music. Phonograph music is preferable to the radio because there are no disruptive commercials. Try to keep the music on for as long as the children are involved with the art. Afterwards, talk over what effect the music had on them. Here are two variations.

• Give the children crayons or fingerpaint and suggest they make freeform or abstract designs done exactly in time to the music.
• Try to find a record of short musical excerpts. Ask the children to each fold one piece of paper in quarters, then smooth it out. Tell them to make different pictures or designs in each quarter, according to the tempo and mood of the music they are hearing. As this may be hard for the younger children, tell them to draw patterned lines of how the music sounds.

Creative Musical Interpretations
Many children are able to react creatively to music without hesitation or inhibition. Others feel lost at first. To assure more ease in their attempts to translate what they hear into rhythmic or dramatic interpretations, here are a few warm-up things they can do:

• When listening to music, disregard any accompanying lyrics and try to extract a mood or message from it. Also, note differences in rhythmic patterns, tempo, volume, tones, pitch, and melody.
• Watch and listen for movement and rhythm in nature, for example the sounds and sights of rain: on pavements, leaves, awnings, window panes, water, metal.
• Listen to manmade sounds to catch rhythm differences, for instance in hammering; sirens; car wheels; ringing telephones; blenders.
• Listen to animal noises: a dog's paw nails on a tile floor: chirping birds; buzzing bees.

Pretend to Music.   Ask each child to decide ahead of time what role he or she will assume, such as:

Animal—elephant; deer; porpoise; crab; seagull; hummingbird
Specialist—ballet, tap, disco, flamenco dancer; tightrope walker; tennis champ; skier; skater
Thing—car; vacuum cleaner; sailboat, kite

Put on music, letting each child dance one at a time. Everyone try to guess what the others are impersonating.

Mood Match.   As the children listen to music, ask them to respond to it by making up original movements and choreography to correspond to the mood it evokes in them. Suggest the following overall reactions, which can express different moods: sadly; happily; exuberantly; slowly; quickly; loudly; lightly; heavily; tentatively; boldly.
Theme Interpretation.   Music often stimulates ideas for an incident or story. Encourage your children to listen for such clues and to try to dance or act out a story line along with the music.
Creative Choreography.   Explain that *choreography* means an original dance set to music. Play music with a lively, strong beat to enable your children to start moving and making up their own dances.

Rhythm Beats
Indoor Rhythms.   Everything we do has some type of rhythm. Suggest to the children that they mark the pattern by clapping or stamping a foot in

accompaniment to your or each other's rhythmic movement at such routine chores as tooth brushing, climbing stairs, beating potatoes, chewing.

Outdoor Romping.   When outside, tell the children to take advantage of large spaces to practice running, leaping, skipping, jogging, jumping, whirling, and swaying to a definite rhythm they can hum, sing, or clap.

Rhythms Instruments

Rhythms instruments can be used creatively either with music or as the rhythmic background for dancing, miming, or exercising. Excellent commercial instruments are available at music and teacher supply stores. Homemade ones are also useful, and making them calls for creativity, too. Help your children produce some of those included below:

Drums.   Almost any kind of round containers can be used, such as coffee cans or oatmeal boxes. For drumheads, tape lids on securely, or cover ends with tightly stretched inner tubing, a double layer of wrapping paper, canvas, heavy linen, oilcloth, or plastic. Secure drumheads with tightly wound elastic bands or strong string. Drumsticks can be made of pencils, dowels, or sticks. Attach a beater of felt; sponge, cork, or rubber to one end.

Tambourine.   Use plates made of paper or aluminum foil. Punch 6 to 8 holes around the edge. Attach to these holes bottle caps with holes punched in them, bells, paper clips, or anything else that will make a sound when the tambourine is tapped and jingled.

Rattles or Marimbas.   These can be made of anything hollow, such as gourds, plastic bottles, spray can tops, film containers, or boxes. Fill with a few small pebbles, dried beans, rice grains, or whatever else will make noise. In the lid, punch a hole just big enough for a small stick to be pushed through to serve as a handle. Paste the stick in the hole, and attach the lid securely with strong household paste or tape.

Sand Blocks.   For these you need two identical pieces of wood about 3″ by 5″. Cover one surface of each with coarse sandpaper. Paste the sandpaper securely, and tape the edges. Handles can be made of spools or large cup hooks attached to the side opposite that with the sandpaper.

Two pieces of styrofoam rubbed together can also be used.

Castanets.   To make these, use either large buttons, walnut shells, plastic bottle lids, or formica sample squares. Attach objects together with loosely tied yarn or string.

Triangles.   Any small metal objects can be used. Test for musical quality when tapping them together; select those that have the best timbre.

Cymbals.   Metal or aluminum foil pie plates clashed together work very well. Handles can be made by placing a hole in the center of each through which you can attach a heavy string or yarn loop.

Strummer.   Use a box, with or without a lid. If you use the lid, cut out a fairly large hole in its center. Place elastic bands across the box, starting at one side with the thinnest and using thicker ones in size graduation.

Organic Rhythms Instruments

Most of the above instruments can be fashioned out of natural materials. When you are in the country, it might be fun for the family to make instant instruments and have a concert.

Stick Drumstick. Any stick can be used to beat against any object: a tree, your shoe, the picnic box, the car seat.

Stone Cymbals. Any two stones or small rocks when banged together make an interesting sound.

Stick Claves. Any pair of twigs or small sticks, with bark removed, will make a nice sound when rubbed together. If you score several lines in one of them and rub it against the other, a different effect results.

Dead Leaf Rustlers. Dead leaves, the sturdier the better, create fascinating sounds when passed over each other.

Shell Castanets. Any two emptied shells will produce sound when hit together; try hazelnuts, acorns, large pits, or sea shells.

Paper-Bag Rattles. Fill paper bags with small objects such as pebbles, bottle caps, jar lids, or plastic cutlery; then close the bags tightly with a secure fastener.

Weed Pipes. Hollow reeds or stems, 3″ to 4″ in circumference, can be tied together in varying lengths about 4″ to 18″. Blow in the large ends. Different lengths will produce different sounds.

Weed Flutes. These can be made from large, hollow reeds or stems 4″ to 18″ long. Whittle out four to eight holes along one surface. When the flute is blown and holes fingered, different tones result.

Singing. There is much room for children to be creative by dramatizing favorite songs, or making up new verses or dance steps to them. The more songs you can add to your family's repertoire, the more opportunities the children will have for thinking of innovative adaptations of them.

Parents do a service to their children when they emphasize how much they value creative activities. Encouraging children to try their skills in a variety of media increases their resourcefulness, eliminates the boredom syndrome, and frees them from overdependency on television.

Still more beneficial experiences for children are outlined in the next chapter.

Far Away from TV—Accentuating Awareness

12

I've saved the best things to do for the last! Deliberate use of the five senses is a no-cost way to have limitless pleasures. The more attuned you are to exposing your sensibilities to the world about you, the less need you have for television entertainment. Compare a fleeting glimpse of a bubbling brook on the small screen to the actual joy of sitting by an authentic one. Envision yourself by your favorite stream, watching the ever-changing water, hearing its music, feeling its coolness on your toes, and smelling the fresh air and foliage. Which experience will mean the most and stay with you the longest in your reservoir of memories? Surely the real scene, no matter how effective television sound effects and background music are. There is something to be said for the excitement of living with the moment, taking advantage of what it has to offer.

In today's highly technical atmosphere, with the current emphasis on doing everything quickly and efficiently, most of us are often too preoccupied to be aware of many of the beautiful subtleties that surround us. Although children are more perceptive of them than adults, traditionally something happens along the path of growing up that dries up even their receptivity. Fortunately you can prevent this from afflicting your children. This chapter emphasizes ways to keep alive their capacity for wonder and surprise as they rejoice in all their senses!

Awareness activities offer many benefits to existence. As you and your family become more sensitized, each person will find:

- life richer and more exciting
- boredom exorcised
- new-found resourcefulness for finding pleasure
- more high moments to balance low ones
- more family compatability through these shared interests
- more satisfaction with life (better mental health!)
- "the best things in life are free"

AWARENESS ACTIVITY

Great Moment

Ensconce yourself in a comfortable spot, close your eyes, and recapture an especially thrilling moment in nature from your past. Think about the outstanding sensations you felt in terms of seeing, hearing, smelling, touching, and possibly tasting. Trace how residues of your raised consciousness at that time have affected you since.

- Recollect how meaningful to you that Great Moment was, and in what ways it still affects you.
- Consider how comparatively rare a Great Moment is in a life time.
- Recall more commonplace experiences analagous to Great Moments, and think of ways to make these happen more frequently to you and your family.

Your children will take to sensitizing experiences like ducks to water. No matter how old they are, probably such things still occur to them naturally. Because their perception is relatively unfettered, look to their leadership as much as you can for discovering new avenues of sensory delights for all to pursue. Encourage them to keep their sense antennae on the alert, explaining that your more aged ones are no longer as sharp as theirs. Talk over and agree that all of you will try to share whatever good things you find.

The outlines below give more details of what to purposefully notice. They are just partial lists, intended to stimulate your ideas.

Sight

Indoors
colors
shapes
fabric/textures
shadows: night/day
contrasts: size; light/dark; soft/hard; loose/tight
outside coming in: light; sun/moon
shadows: moving/stationary
reflections: color tone; sunlit dust; rain on windows; TV's light
   and movement
Outdoors
colors at different times of day and night
shapes: still and moving; through fog, rain
all aspects of nature
shadows: size; shape
contrasts: size; shape; color; movement
reflections: at different times

Sound

Indoors
feet, hands on different surfaces
customary activity noises in house
noises heard from outside: birds, garden sprays
people: voices; use of things
occasional noises: phone, appliances
cooking, washing, cleaning noises
pets
Outdoors
street; air; distant
while in car, on sidewalk
nature: birds; during storms; wind; animals
water: rain; surf; running streams
people: voices; working noises

Smell

Indoors
each room of house/garage/barn/woodshed
cooking odors
in school; beauty parlor; MD's office
fabrics; wood; plastic; hair; fur

Outdoors
  backyard
  city; country
  sidewalk; street
  nature: after rain; fields; woods
General
  fresh/stale/tainted
  fire: smouldering; burning
  dry/moist
  concentrated/diluted

Touch
  temperatures: hot/cold/tepid/freezing
  textures: rough/smooth; hard/soft; sharp/dull
  wet/moist/damp/dry

Taste
  before and after cooking
  bland/sharp/seasoned/spicy; sweet/sour
  aftertaste
  compared to odor of same thing

It will be easy to explain to your family what accentuating awareness means. You can describe the activities in this chapter as "awareness adventures," a process of opening to and filling up your total selves with sensations of every possible type. Here is a sample you can use, an awareness adventure with the wind, that involves all the senses except taste; your children might find some way to include that one, too. The wind's effects can be:

Seen on trees; grass; clouds; water; awnings; drapes; people's clothes; hair; pushing against bodies; scattering leaves and litter.
Heard moaning; gusting; through trees; against windows; through vents and drafts; down chimneys.
Felt against bodies: caressing; pushing; cooling; freezing; whipping clothes and hair.
Smelled as it carries smoke; salt spray; barbecue, industrial, and farm odors.

Another important component to awareness is its influence on moods. Combined with or as a result of the bodily sensations we experience, our reactions can run the gamut from exhilaration to pensiveness. The wind, for example, can play many tricks on people, plunging them into nostalgia, making them restless or tense, frightening or saddening them.

Sense Searches

Sense Searches are concentrated efforts to be attuned to a variety of awareness experiences each day. Each person can keep an outline record or short diary of what he or she notices, and when. A composite chart posted on a bulletin board is handy for the entire family's use and sharing.

Shared Sensations

Shared Sensations are more in-depth evaluations than Sense Searches. Do them frequently for the pleasure they bring everyone. Take turns (you be first) selecting something upon which everyone concentrates, afterwards sharing their impressions about it. The choices can be anything related to the senses, like looking at a pretty object; listening to music; smelling flowers; wading; tasting exotic food. As you talk over these experiences, suggest different approaches for examining them, such as:

- why and how they appeal
- what associations they hold
- why they are of value
- if they are reminiscent or symbolic of anything
- what mood they evoke

Mystery Tray

Prepare ahead of time a tray containing several unusual things to touch, hear, smell, and taste, like a satin handkerchief, a small bell, a sachet, and raisins soaked in fruit juice. Darken the room and put on some quiet background music. Ask each child to come in separately and to close his or her eyes. Help the child slowly savour each thing, taking time to have the child describe his or her reactions. After everyone has had a turn, tell them to open their eyes and look at what they felt, heard, smelled, and tasted. Encourage your children to set up Mystery Trays for each other and you.

Week of September 17th.	
Monday	▷ Bird chirping - Tom ▷ Hamburger cooking - Dad ▷ Dew on grass - Sue
Tuesday	▷ Wet grass - everyone ▷ Zooming cars on ▷ Window shutters - Mom freeway - Dad ▷ Dripping leaves - Tom
Wednesday	▷ Burning leaves - Mom ▷ Lentil soup - ▷ Sunset - Sue Sue and Dad ▷ Bicycle wheels - Tom
Thursday	▷ Neon lights downtown - Tom ▷ Fire engines - Sue ▷ Carrot cake baking - everyone ▷ School yard at recess - Tom
Friday	▷ Fried fish and potatoes - Tom ▷ New mown lawn - Dad ▷ Rainbow - Sue
Saturday	▷ Soft kitten fur - Sue ▷ Pot roast - everyone ▷ Symphony on radio - Mom and Dad.

Sunday	▷ Cold lake water - Dad and Tom
	   ▷ Picnic basket - everyone
	▷ Country smells - everyone
	   ▷ Rough rocks - Sue
	▷ Pine needles on ground - Mom

Sample Sense Search Chart

Sense Capades

Sense Capades are imaginary trips to different places and spaces that can be described verbally or in writing by one person or several people together. Each person selects a desirable spot and pretends to be there, explaining whatever sensations seem appropriate for that setting. The following ideas can be starters for your voyages of escape:

- in a forest of filtered sun and shade
- on a cloud
- on the crest of a wave
- in tall grass
- on a sailboat

Awareness Hunt

Awareness Hunt is a game that can be played anywhere and all of the time, by everyone in the family, yourself included. Each player decides on one thing per day or week to be on the alert for. The object is to discover it in as many as possible places, variations, forms, uses, or contexts. To keep track of these, it might help to list them as they are found. Here are some examples:

- Shape—straight or zigzag line; oval; triangle
- Sound—dripping; humming motor; insect buzz
- Touch—cool metal; slippery; coarse
- Smell—exotic; pungent; perfumed
- Taste—pronounced; herbal

Mix and Match

Cut out or draw pictures of a variety of items, like a boat, milk carton, or baby carriage. If your children are readers, you can skip the pictures and just write a short description of each thing on a separate piece of paper. For the first few go-arounds, tell each child to select two items to pair for the creation of something *new* and *different;* for instance, a boat and baby carriage could be combined to form a floating carriage. Each description should include as many references to the five senses as possible. For variation, the children can pick the pictures or word cards at random, or you can ask them to figure out how the combinations could result in something like the following:

- a beautiful scene/sight
- a soothing sound
- a woodsy smell
- something nice to touch
- something tasty to eat

Fancy Fantasies

To add spice to actual experiences, suggest that each child make up (to tell or write) descriptions of the five senses in imagined situations, projecting themselves into such nonhuman "skins" as: a butterfly; the family car; worn-out shoes; an overstuffed handbag; a bar of bath soap.

Written Sensations

Your children might like to collect their awareness experiences in written form, perhaps putting them in such catergories as: routine/usual, unusual, extraordinary; nature, indoors; seasonal; and so forth. Whenever possible, encourage them to make original drawings to enhance such descriptions. Bound books of each child's impressions are treasured volumes to own!

Becoming more purposefully conscious of awareness experiences takes some practice, but once started it can gain momentum that lasts forever. Such pleasures compete with television's artificiality and are easily available as diversions from TV's attraction.

In the chapter to follow, I suggest how you can evaluate your family's reaction to the *TV Turn On/Off Project* and include some programs and resources specifically concerned with children and television.

A Look Ahead: TV in Your Family's Future

13

It is time to think about how large a portion of your family life you want your family to devote to television from now on. Your use of the suggestions in previous chapters may have helped you to form new opinions about what TV does and means to you and each family member. Hopefully your children are no longer victimized by it, but have learned to cope more effectively with what they watch and are able to enjoy alternative activities as well. No matter to what degree each one of you became involved in the *TV Turn On/Off Project,* in all probability your attitudes about the use of television have been influenced.

Ask each of your children to write down or talk over with you their responses to the Postquestionnaire below, and to compare them to what they wrote on the Prequestionnaire in Chapter 2. You may all be in for some surprises when you note the changes that have occurred.

HELPFUL THINGS TO DO

Postquestionnaire

Personal Use of and Reactions to TV   Date:_____

How much time I spend watching daily:
Former programs eliminated:

New programs tried:
New programs seen on regular basis:
Alternative activities to TV viewing:
How I feel about TV:

what it does for me
what it inspires me to do
what it waylays me from doing

Do I feel differently about TV now in any way?

Use the last Awareness Activity to crystallize your reactions.

AWARENESS ACTIVITY

Project Overview

- Were some or all of my goals met?
- What were the most successful Helpful Things to Do?
- What were the least successful Helpful Things to Do?
- What new insights did I gain?
- Have my children's TV behaviors changed in any of the following areas? The ability to:

  - distinguish fact from fiction
  - understand content
  - evaluate programs more critically
  - discuss what they view
  - cut down on viewing time

- How do I feel about TV now in relation to myself; in relation to each family member; as a source of information and entertainment.

Rejoice in whatever improvements have occurred in your family's use of TV. This might be just the right moment to plan a family party to celebrate the progress you have made. By so honoring your individual and collective conquests of television—your friendly enemy—you reinforce incentives needed to maintain your continuing resistance to its magnetic pull.

Here are some ideas for a party.

HELPFUL THINGS TO DO

Victory Over TV Day

- Cover all TV screens.
- Make victory banners like:

- Congratulations to Us!
- We Cured Ourselves of TeeVeeitis
- Free to Be without TV!
- We're a TV-Liberated Family
- Down with TeeVeeitis
- TV-Friend not Foe
- TV-Partner not Dictator

- Plan an elaborate picnic or especially good dinner, including everyone's favorite foods.
- After eating, do something together like:

  - Read outloud.
  - Play games.
  - Go for a walk.
  - Listen to the record player or radio.
  - Talk about your future plans for wise use of the TV set to get rid of its unwanted influences. Make up a chant to vent your resentments about the problems it has caused your family.

- Leave up a few banners after the party as reminders.
- Plan future celebrations on a regular basis.

To keep their minds open and curious, keep on encouraging your children to try other ideas and experiences, especially first-hand experiences in which they search out and discover things for themselves. Continue to wean them away from dependency on using TV as a background to other activities or, even more importantly, as a surrogate "companion" during free time. Always remind them of how exciting the world can be away from the perimeters of the television set.

I do not want to give you the impression that I consider all television of questionable value for family viewing. On the contrary, excellent children's and family programs have always been available, with more appearing than ever before on the major commercial and public broadcasting networks.

Although it is risky to list programs, as their scheduling is subject to change, and new ones crop up all the time, here are some good ones you might watch for.

ABC

Afterschool Specials—for upper elementary children
Weekend Specials
Superfriends Hour
Kids are People Too—ten- to fourteen-year-olds
Animals, Animals, Animals
Schoolhouse Rock

CBS
Captain Kangaroo—for preschoolers
Children's Film Festival
Fat Albert and the Cosby Kids
In the News
Kidsworld—for intermediate
The CBS Library
Thirty Minutes
Razzmatazz

NBC
Special Treat
Afternoon Specials
Hot Hero Sandwich
Metric Marvels
The Junior Hall of Fame

PBS
For preschoolers
Sesame Street
I-Land Treasure
Mister Rogers' Neighborhood
For primary-school-aged children
The Young at Art—2nd and 3rd graders
The Folk Book
The Art Cart—Kindergarten through 3rd graders
Math Country—2nd and 3rd graders
Music and Me—3rd and 4th graders
Under the Yellow Balloon—2nd and 3rd graders
Word Feathers—1st graders
For older elementary-school-aged children
3-2-1 Contact—3rd through 6th graders
Thinkabout—5th and 6th graders
The Electric Company
Once Upon a Classic
Vision On
Villa Allegre and Carrascolendas—bilingual and bicultural
Infinity Factory
Rebop
Zoom
Feelings—children 8 years and older

On Various Channels
Big Blue Marble
Dusty's Treehouse

The Froozles
Hot Fudge
Kidsworld
Vegetable Soup
Changing Places

Cable TV
Warner Amex's "Nickelodeon
United Artists "Calliope"

To keep abreast of what is available for children, we suggest that you frequently phone your local network program directors to check on the scheduling of children's shows. Write the information down on your calendar so that you can plan ahead for family viewing.

Another way to learn about program schedules is to write to the children's program directors at the networks. Here is a list of network addresses:

ABC-TV
1330 Avenue of the Americas
New York, N.Y. 10019

CBS Television Network
51 W. 52nd Street
New York, N.Y. 10020

NBC-TV
30 Rockefeller Plaza
New York, N.Y. 10020

Public Broadcasting Service
475 L'Enfant Plaza West, S.W.
Washington, D.C. 20024

Still another source of program information comes from television columns in newspapers and periodicals. Often previews and reviews in these are very helpful. Make a habit of reading them.

Many organizations have also adopted the custom of evaluating and listing television programs appropriate for family viewing. Below are some of them:

Agency for Instructional Television
Box A
Bloomington, Indiana 47402

National Assoc. for Better Broadcasting
P.O. Box 43640
Los Angeles, Calif. 90043

National Citizens Committee For Broadcasting
1028 Connecticut Ave., N.W.
Washington, D.C. 20036

National Parent-Teacher Assoc.
TV Action Center
700 N. Rush Street
Chicago, Ill. 60611

Parent Participation Workshops
c/o Teachers Guides to Television
699 Madison Ave.
New York, N.Y. 10021

Television Information Office
745 5th Avenue
New York, N.Y. 10022

Prime Time School Television
120 S. LaSalle Street
Chicago, Illinois 60603

National Assoc. for the Education of Young Children
Media Committee
1834 Connecticut Ave., N.W.
Washington, D.C. 20009

Project Focus
1061 Brooks Avenue
St. Paul, Minn. 55113

TV and Movie Facts for Parents
Box A–4
1345 3rd Avenue
New York, N.Y. 10021

Some of you may want to become even more actively involved in the crusade to guide parents to more careful attention to their children's exposure to television. I suggest that first you search in your immediate communities to find out if there are any already established groups working towards similar goals. If not, you may want to start your own.

Below is a list of some of the organizations concerned with better use of television with children. Send for their materials to help you gain a clearer perspective of what is being done and what you can do.

Action for Children's Television
46 Austin Street
Newtonville, Mass. 02160

Center for Early Education and Development
Room 226, Institute of Child Development
51 E. River Road
Minneapolis, Minn. 55455

Council of Children, Media & Merchandising
1346 Connecticut Ave., N.W.
Washington, D.C. 20036

Gessell Institute in Child Development
TV Information Center
745 5th Avenue
New York, N.Y. 10022

Institute for Visual Learning
1061 Brooks Avenue
St. Paul, Minn. 55113

Minneapolis Children's Health Center
2525 Chicago Avenue
Minneapolis, Minn. 55455

National Academy of Television Arts & Sciences
110 West 57th Street
New York, N.Y. 10019

National Citizens Committee for Broadcasting
1530 P Street
Washington, D.C. 20005

National Assoc. for the Education of Young Children
1834 Connecticut Ave. N.W.
Washington, D.C. 20009

Television Awareness Training
Media Action Research Center, Inc.
475 Riverside Drive
New York, N.Y. 10027

Television Resources, Inc.
Box 6712
Chicago, Ill. 60680

The Yale University Family Television Research and
Consultation Center
Box 11 A
Yale Station
New Haven, Conn. 06520

Government Agencies
ERIC Clearinghouse On Early Childhood Education
805 W. Pennsylvania Avenue
Urbana, Ill. 61801

Federal Communications Commission
Consumer Assistance Office, Room 258
1919 M Street, N.W.
Washington, D.C. 20580

Federal Trade Commission
Pennsylvania Ave. & 6th St., N.W.
Washington, D.C. 20580

Senate Subcomm. on Communications
Russell Senate Office Building
Room B 333
Washington, D.C. 20515

House Subcomm. on Communications
Rayburn House Office Building
Room B 333
Washington, D.C. 20515

Corporation for Public Broadcasting
1111 16th St., N.W.
Washington, D.C. 20036

More and more groups are forming to publish a variety of materials
parents can use to help children make better use of television. Listed here
are those most appropriate for children up to about twelve years:

Association for Childhood Education International
3615 Wisconsin Ave., N.W.
Washington, D.C. 20016

Child Study Assoc. of America, Inc.
9 East 89th Street
New York, N.Y. 10028

Center for Understanding Media
267 West 25th Street
New York, N.Y. 10001

Children's Television Workshop
Community Education Services Division
One Lincoln Place
New York, N.Y. 10023

Project Focus
1061 Brooks Avenue
St. Paul, Minn. 55113

Southwest Educational Development Laboratory
211 East 7th Street
Austin, Texas 78701

Now you are well equipped to take advantage of television in the best possible ways and to help your family feast at its bounteous table. Your continued care in guiding your children to use it appropriately is an invaluable orientation to the electronic wonders that will be available in the future. Complex plans for tomorrow's improved communications technology are on today's drawing boards. Ahead for you, and even more for your children, grandchildren, and *their* grandchildren, are fantastic devices most of which are sophisticated offshoots of the contemporary television we know.

Turn now to the last chapter, which surveys the current climate of opinion and some research findings about television's impact on children and family life.

TV - The Powerful Demon-Angel

Although this book is primarily a how-to-do-it book, it is important to touch on the current climate of opinion and include a brief overview of the questions researchers raise about children and television. The concern about TV's effect on them is growing in scope and intensity as more and more research reports and experts' opinions surface. Hardly a week goes by without the appearance of a newspaper or magazine article containing alarming information about what is happening to our TV-viewing children. We are being alerted to the potential damages they may be suffering in all areas of their development: intellectual, physical, psychological, and social.

Meanwhile, the battle about changing TV programming is waged on more fronts. Groups such as Action for Children's Television and the National Parent Teacher Association are stating their opinions more loudly and consistently across the nation. Hearings, conferences, and public forums are becoming more commonplace as people's awareness and sense of commitment to children's welfare turn them into activists. The lines are now drawn between consumers of TV's fare and those who are involved in its production, a large conglomerate of networks, producers, and advertisers.

At the moment this War of the Airwaves is not much of a contest due to the unevenness of the armies engaged in it. The citizens' groups are no match for the combined dollar-based power of the networks, producers, advertising agencies, and sponsors. Reports from the front appear weekly in Nielsen ratings. These barometerlike readings seem to dwarf the significance, at least momentarily, of the research findings and experts' opinions that the viewers' groups are using for ammunition. Behind the battlefront, TV fare continues much as usual, if not even more sensational (a euphemism for any new form of violence, sex, or inanity that might be appearing) as programmers search for innovative formats to attract and maintain their audiences.

The more serious implications of the controversy are the hidden ones. These are the insidious effects of TV viewing as a long-term habit. Even though the battle cries concentrate on children, research intimates that some of the recent changes in society at large may have been generated, at least partially, by an increased use of TV during the past several decades. Current statistics reveal that 98 percent of all American homes have at least one TV set that is turned on an average of six hours per day. Until it is proved innocent, TV is now stigmatized as one of the main reasons for growing psychosocial unrest in our country. Accusatory voices criticize TV's role in relation to nonreading children, inattentive children, violence, working mothers, broken homes, sexual mores, sensationalism in news reports, materialism, promotional methods in political campaigns, and innumerable other aspects of human behavior that have undergone rapid alterations.

It may come as a surprise to many that researchers gave warnings about television's possible effects years ago, almost from the outset of television's growing popularity. One of the first major reports came from England in 1958, based on a study made by Himmelweit and coworkers. Their findings were inconclusive due to many variables over which they had no control, but they did note many incipient changes in children's behavior.

The Himmelweit study concerned itself with the cause-and-effect aspects of television on children who were habitual viewers. In general terms, what was happening to them? At what ages were they most impressionable? How much information did they absorb and retain, and at what age? How important had TV become to them? As a main use of their free time, what was the significance of what it was displacing? How much and why were they using it? What effect did it have on their ability to fantasize? How much did they understand of what they saw and heard? Did TV confuse their ability to differentiate between reality and fantasy? What kind of and how much impact did TV have on their beliefs and attitudes about people's behavior, and some of the realities of life? In what ways might TV be unsettling them, causing them fears and anxieties? How meaningful were some of the things they were learning? As much of the learning stimuli appeared to them out of context, how much of that could they conceptualize and retain? In terms of incidental or subliminal learning, what kinds of facts were most impressionable to them? What might be the cumulative effect on them of exposure to television?

It was found that the least emotionally and socially mature children were the most deeply affected. Depending on what they brought of their own emotions and experiences to television, each child had a different reaction and remembered what was of unique consequence to him or her when viewing. Many children were upset by what they saw, particularly in relation to portrayed family problems, which often disturbed them as much as or more than scenes of violence. The researchers found an overall loss of innocence of childhood and noted that continual use of TV, especially serial-type programs, can change children's attitudes.

In 1961 a report of a study similar in many respects to the Himmelweit report was published here in America by Schramm and others, entitled *Television in the Lives of Our Children.* Again, the results were inconclusive, but as with the English results, there was evidence that television had a predominently negative effect on heavy users, and it was suspected of causing behavioral changes to a greater or lesser degree in *most* child viewers, with the exception in some instances of very bright youngsters. The main thrust of this study was to try to determine why children watch television and what they get out of it. The question was raised as to how and what they were learning, particularly in terms of the importance of some of the incidental learning as opposed to intentional learning opportunities provided by TV. The quandary of the mixture of fantasy and reality was studied, with emphasis on what if any confusion it might lead to in relation to children's ability to do problem solving in real life. The researchers were also concerned with what TV might do to children's desire and ability to socialize. They attempted to find out how pervasive an influence television is on children's total development.

Among the findings of this study was the fact that TV isolates children from significant others, especially peers, and that it encourages withdrawal from reality, leading to possible addiction. It was also determined that television, to which children are exposed earliest and for the greatest amounts of time, colors their expectations for the other mass media, reading materials most importantly, making these less desirable.

At the end of the report the authors raised a provocative question for future researchers that holds interest for us all. It is as pertinent today as in 1961 and may even be more important now as a review of what has happened to TV in the intervening years. The authors asked "whether television degrades the American ethos, or reflects it. Is television an amusement park distortion mirror reflecting a crazy caricature of ourselves—or is it a clear and accurate reflection of what we as a nation are and want to be?"[1]

By Congressional request in 1969 the Department of Health, Education and Welfare started a special investigatory program under the auspices of the Surgeon General's Scientific Advisory Committee on Television and Social Behavior. The results of the studies revealed a definite link between children's viewing and their behavior, both antisocial and prosocial. Recommendations for the improvement of both production and use of television were inconclusive and tentative, for the same reason as with previous research: the variables are too vast; so many aspects of human behavior have yet to be examined. A statement summarizing this dilemma comes from "Television and the Behavior of Preschool Children" by Harold W. Stevenson: "When we begin to compare what we need to know with what we do know, our past efforts at research seem puny indeed. Television is a powerful medium, capable of introducing enormous change. A vast amount of research must be conducted before its power can result in positive influences on children's lives rather than stultifying and eroding influences on the creativity and vitality of the young children of the nation."[2]

More recent research done at the Yale Child Study Center by Drs. Jerome and Dorothy Singer and their associates has concentrated on television's effect on preschool children. One of the main concerns of the Singers has to do with children's imaginative play. They have found that unless adult intervention aids children to make fuller use of what stimulation they receive from television to enhance their own creativity, this facet of their development can be impaired.

Why have research reports gone unheeded by the general public? Part of the reason for this may be that their findings are threatening to the status quo, and people feel helpless and frustrated when they relate them to their personal lives. Added to this is the fact that the reports are not easily accessible, and most people would find them difficult if not boring to read. So once the findings have been noted in the press, then they are forgotten by the majority of people.

Nor has much attention been paid to the books on this subject that have appeared fairly regularly in recent years. *Television's Child* by Norman Morris was published as long ago as 1971. One of the most disquieting revelations in this book was the apathy among the teachers and parents concerning what television might be doing to their students and children. Notwithstanding their apparent lack of concern, Mr. Morris's survey reinforced his suppositions about some of TV's detrimental effects. Among the many issues he covered are these: How much of what they are seeing and hearing are children swallowing whole, in total acceptance of its validity? To what extent are parent-child relationships being diffused by the intrusion of television and its apparent importance to child viewers? Is there a lessening of human relationships because of this; are children and parents becoming somewhat isolated from one another despite the fact that they dwell in the same home? And what about the time children lose when they watch TV? Is it irretrievable time in terms of their development?

Another book based on interviews with hundreds of families, teachers, and child specialists is *The Plug-In Drug: Television, Children, and the Family* by Marie Winn. Perhaps the most forceful part of Mrs. Winn's message is her indictment against parents for the way in which they have abused their children in order to benefit themselves. She accuses them of turning the TV set into a constant and convenient babysitter. She touches a

raw nerve in most of us, as rare is the parent today who hasn't at one time
or another told a child to remove his or her annoying self to the television
set. Mrs. Winn's book is anxiety provoking; that was her intent in writing it.
Her following comment summarizes her feelings: "Surely there can be no
more insidious a drug than one that you must administer to others in order
to achieve an effect on yourself."[3]

As this is being written, it is almost impossible to quote valid statistics of
what is occurring to people because of television; the statistics keep changing. In general terms effects are noticeable, however. More and more TV
sets are being purchased; it is no longer unusual for each family member to
have his or her own set. Dinner time in many homes has become a scene of
separation, with family members sitting in front of different TV sets, eating
TV dinners off of trays. The average number of hours per day that are spent
either in front of TV or with TV turned on are increasing. Children's use of
television is on the rise, and younger and younger children are exposed to
TV, either propped up in front of the screen by their parents or able to view
the set from their cribs or playpens. The amount of violence portrayed on
television, from the milder forms of battling cartoon figures to the more
realistic portrayal of people attacking one another, is becoming uncon-
scionable *despite* the protests of PTA and other activist groups. Meanwhile
the growing violence in our society seems to be commensurate with the
amount showing up on the TV screen. Perhaps the most shocking cause for
alarm in reference to this is the rising violence perpetrated by younger and
younger children.

Repercussions associated with television amount to a grim picture in
education on all levels. Nationwide, reading scores for elementary and
secondary children continue to go down; the number of partially illiterate
college students is increasing. Classroom teachers are finding it harder each
year to establish a healthy learning environment, no matter for what age
students they are responsible. It is not only the discipline problem that con-
fronts them, but the imperative to capture and hold children's attention.
Teachers complain that children "turn us off" very easily, seem restless and
apathetic. Many of the tried and true tricks of motivation no longer are effective. Educators find themselves in competition with television's effects,
and they often feel that they are losing or have already lost the struggle for
children's minds. This change in children's behavior finds them baffled and
in many instances unable to cope. The lag between the recognition of the
problem facing today's teachers and what to do about it is creating havoc in
an ever-growing number of classrooms.

Parents are quick to accuse teachers of bad instruction without realizing
the part that they unwittingly play in this serious situation. Daniel N. Fader
et al. sum it up succinctly: "students . . . have grown accustomed to the
absence of attention given or received in the familial structure engendered
by six hours of daily television in the average home. No one, I think, can

now know the full meaning of this extraordinary influence upon our North American culture, but anyone can know what this social change means and has meant to the teaching of writing in our schools."[4] To the "writing" one can add all of the other subjects taught.

Although people are beginning to become uneasy about television and children, they probably are not yet angry or disgruntled enough. For the most part the upheaval is in the blaming stage; everyone looks to someone else to pinpoint the cause. What is constantly being overlooked in the barrage of accusations is the positive potential for TV's use with children, and adults, too. The one exception is the universal acknowledgment that instructional television used in classrooms has proved to be an effective teaching device. Unfortunately, most critics of television either ignore or make little of the increasing number of worthwhile children and family programs appearing on both commercial and public broadcasting networks.

It is paradoxical, however, that even though more people are aware that television might have a bad long-range influence on children, most parents are slow to associate that aspect in relation to their own children. When asked their opinions about television and children, they usually answer that the children enjoy it so much, or they can't get the children away from the set, or children learn from it. When pressed for specifics concerning *what* the children learn, parents usually can only generalize, except for those with preschoolers who watch "Sesame Street." These latter parents believe that their children have picked up a lot of direct learnings from that program. In terms of older children, parents refer to educational programs about animal life, science, etc., and then confess that their children are not as enthusiastic about such programs as they are about sitcoms, game shows, and other "kidult" programs that were intended primarily for adult viewers but are seen by children as well. In essence, the average parent sees television as a recreation for the family and does not question too deeply what other kinds of effects it might have, except for the "gimme" syndrome brought on by the incessant stream of commercials. Many parents do resent this part of TV. Those who score violence on TV as being undesirable admit that they have difficulty in completely preventing their children's exposure to it, as there is so much being shown.

Like everything else, television has its good side as well as its bad. Everyone agrees with this. For those who were growing up before its advent, it seemed like a miracle, and still does for many. Today's children take it for granted; it is something dependable that has always been in their world. For everyone, young or old, it has taken a prominent place in daily existence. It has something to offer for every kind of taste and is an unending source of learning, amusement, escape, instant information, or whatever else one might seek at the moment. It extends horizons and expands knowledge. It informs, entertains, keeps people up-to-date on happenings big and small, makes them think, tickles their imaginations, and brings them beauty in many forms. What a shame to condemn television. Everyone really ought to smarten up and learn to use it more wisely. I hope this book has helped you to do so!

1.   Wilbur Schramm et al., *Television in the Lives of Our Children* (Stanford, Ca.: Stanford University Press, 1961), p. 194.

2.   Surgeon General's Scientific Advisory Committee, *Television and Social Behavior, Reports and Papers,* vol. II (Washington, D.C.: U.S. Department of Health, Education, and Welfare, 1969), p. 369.

3.   Marie Winn, *The Plug-In Drug: Television, Children, and the Family* (New York: The Viking Press, 1977), p. 11.

4.   Daniel N. Fader et al., *The New Hooked on Books* (New York: G.P. Putnams's Sons, 1976), p. 44.

Appendix A

Suggested Readings
More Suggested Readings
Books for Children About TV

Suggested Readings

ARLEN, MICHAEL J. *The View From Highway 1.* New York: Farrar, Straus and Giroux, 1976.
  Essays on every aspect of current television fare, providing insight into its role in our communications-conscious society. Of special interest is the essay "Kidvid."

BROWN, LES. *Television: The Business Behind the Box.* New York: Harcourt Brace Jovanovich, 1971.
  A journalist's anecdotal, detailed documentary of a year in the television industry.

COMSTOCK, GEORGE. *Effects of Television on Children. What Is the Evidence?* Santa Monica, Ca.: The Rand Corp., 1975.
  Paper presented at 1975 Telecommunications Policy Research Conference.

COWAN, GEOFFREY. *See No Evil.* New York: Simon & Schuster, 1979.
  An informative, dispassionate overview of the inner workings of the networks and of television's power as a communications medium.

FREEMAN, DON. *Eyes as Big as Cantaloupes: An Irreverent Look at TV.* San Diego, Ca.: Joyce Press, 1978.
  Comments on the best and worst of TV programs, written in a humorous style by a TV editor and commentator.

GOLDSEN, ROSE K. *The Show and Tell Machine: How Television Works and Works You Over.* New York: The Dial Press, 1977.
A thorough survey of television as an industry controlled by a relatively small number of decision makers, and geared solely to making money. An eye-opening account of television production as viewed from behind the scenes, and the psychic pollution it spreads.

JOHNSON, NICHOLAS. *How To Talk Back To Your Television Set.* Boston: Little, Brown & Co. 1967.
A thoughtful, in-depth look at television as a powerful force in American life by a former FCC Commissioner. Although written over a decade ago, questions raised in this book are still of interest today.

KAVANAUGH, DORRIET, ed. *Listen to Us: The Children's Express Report.* New York: Workman Publishing, 1979.
An invaluable record of teenagers' reports on television's effect on them. Their revelations should be carefully considered in terms of all children's TV viewing.

KAYE, EVELYN. *The Family Guide to Children's Television: What to Watch, What to Miss, What to Change and How to Do It.* New York: Pantheon Books, 1974.
Offering just what the subtitles imply, this useful book for parents suggests practical ideas for how to improve children's use of television.

KAYE, EVELYN. *How To Treat TV with TLC: The ACT Guide to Children's Television.* Boston: Beacon Press, 1979.
This is a practical book that provides current research and federal regulatory activities as well as a resource directory, a speaker's planning kit, and a "short course" in broadcasting.

LESSER, HARVEY. *Television and the Preschool Child.* New York: Academic Press, 1979.
This book, concerning children of six and seven as well as preschoolers, is based on research related to television viewing in four areas: reasoning; language and thought; image and reality; structure and function of mentality.

LEWIS, GREGG. *Telegarbage: What You Can Do about Sex and Violence on TV.* New York: Thomas Nelson Inc., 1977.
Directed at Christian readers, this book offers valuable information for all readers on the "hows" of TV and its effect on our culture.

LIEBERT, ROBERT M. et al. *The Early Window: Effects of Television on Children and Youth.* New York: Pergamon Press, Inc. 1973.
A brief account of research on what children learn from viewing and how it affects their psychological and social behavior. The main theme centers on how television relates to children's attitudes, development, and behavior, with an exploration of the political and social questions raised by these findings.

MANKIEWICZ, FRANK and SWERDLOW, JOEL. *Remote Control Television and the Manipulation of American Life.* New York: Times Books, 1979.
The authors take a close look at children's behavior as a result of television viewing and contend that it is negatively affected.

MELODY, WILLIAM H. *Children's Television: The Economics of Exploitation.* New Haven: Yale University Press, 1973.
Tracing the history of television as it relates to children, the author scores some of the bad effects its commercialism has on them.

MORRIS, NORMAN. *Television's Child.* Boston: Little, Brown & Co. 1971.
An interesting and readable survey of television and its effect on children, with special emphasis on the psychoemotional ramifications of programming and commercials. Included is an analysis of the major networks' and producers' approach to programming for children. Ideas for how to make TV a better experience are suggested.

POTTER, ROSEMARY L. *New Season: The Positive Use of Commercial Television With Children.* Columbus, Ohio: Merrill, 1976.
A practical book, written for teachers but also useful for parents, on how to take advantage of commercial television to improve children's writing, reading, and learning skills.

RUTSTEIN, NAT. *"Go Watch TV!" What and How Much Should Children Really Watch?* New York: Sheed & Ward, 1974.
A psychosocial overview of the effect of television on children, with documentation of the potential harm it can do.

SCHRAMM, WILBUR et al. *Television in the Lives of Our Children.* Stanford, Ca.: Stanford University Press, 1961.
Although published in 1961, this is a fascinating book based on research findings, many of which are still applicable today. Comparatively easy to read, this book can give useful insights to parents. Extensive appendices help elucidate the mechanisms and results of the research.

SINGER, DOROTHY G. and SINGER, JEROME L. *Partners in Play.* New York: Harper & Row, 1978.
Stressing the need for children to have ample opportunities to use their imaginations, the authors make suggestions for how to use television to stimulate rather than cut off children's imaginations.

WINN, MARIE. *The Plug-In Drug: Television, Children and the Family.* New York: The Viking Press, 1977.
Based on interviews with hundreds of families, teachers, and child specialists, this book shows what can happen to children's abilities and behavior if they are not guided in their use of television.

more suggested readings

ADLER, RICHARD and CATER, DOUGLAS, eds. *Television as a Cultural Force.* New York: Praeger, 1976.

ADLER, RICHARD et al. *Research on the Effects of Commercial Advertising on Children.* Washington, D.C.: U.S. Government Printing Office, 1977.

ASSOC. FOR CHILDHOOD EDUCATION INTERNATIONAL. *Children and Television: Television's Impact on the Child.* Washington, D.C., 1967.

BENEDICK, JEANNE. *Television Works Like This,* 4th ed. New York: McGraw-Hill, 1965.

COOK, THOMAS D. et al. *Sesame Street Revisited.* New York: Russell Sage Foundation, 1975.

CORBETT, SCOTT. *What Makes TV Work?* Boston: Little, Brown & Co. 1965.

DE FRANCO, ELLEN B. *Alternatives to TV.* Englewood Cliffs, N.J.: Prentice-Hall Learning Sytems, Inc., 1978.

FRANK, JOSETTE, ed. *Television: How to Use It Wisely with Children.* New York: Child Study Assoc. of America, 1976.

HALLORAN, J.D. and ELLIOTT, P.R. *Television for Children and Young People.* New York: International Publishers Service, 1970.

LESSER, HARVEY, ed. *Television and the Preschool Child: A Psychological Theory of Instruction and Curriculum Development.* New York: Academic Press, 1977.

LESHAN, EDA and POLK, L. *The Incredible Television Machine.* New York: Macmillan Publishing Co., 1977.

LOGAN, BEN, ed. *Television Awareness Training.* New York: Media Action Research Center, 1977.

MAYER, MARTIN. *About Television.* New York: Harper & Row, 1972.

WINICK, MARIANN P. *Television Experience: What Children See.* People and Communications Series 6. New York: Russell Sage Foundation, 1979.

books for children about TV

BEAL, GEARE. *See Inside a Television Studio.* New York: Warwick Press, 1977.
A comprehensive, illustrated outline of how television works. Appropriate for the upper elementary aged child.

STODDARD, EDWARD. *Television,* rev. ed. New York: Watts, 1970.
A clearly outlined explanation of how television works, appropriate for the older elementary aged child who is interested in electronics.

TANNENBAUM, HAROLD E. *We Read About Television and How It Works.* St. Louis: Webster Publishing Co., 1960.
A brief, easy explanation of how television works, appropriate for the primary aged child.

Appendix B

Film Rental Resources on Television Education

Film Rental Resources on Television Education

Action for Children's Television
46 Austin Street
Newtonville, Mass. 02160

Churchill Films
662 No. Robertson Blvd.
Los Angeles, Calif. 90069

Project Focus
1061 Brooks Avenue
St. Paul, Minn. 55113

Pyramid Films
2801 Colorado Avenue
Santa Monica, Calif. 90401

Television Awareness Training
Media Action Research Center, Inc.
475 Riverside Drive
New York, N.Y. 10027

Vision Films
P.O. Box 48896
Los Angeles, Calif. 90048